**glish muffins
ted here**
*ue between
Street and
)th Street
t 20th Street
nd 9th Avenues*

**The disco where the
most beautiful people
danced the night away**
*254 West 54th Street,
between 8th Avenue
and Broadway*

**The first pedestrian
caused by an automobile in the
United States happened here**
Central Park West and 74th Street

The Cotton Club
*Times Square location
(from 1936 to 1940)
200 West 48th Street*

**Where a hail of hot lead
cut down mob boss
Albert Anastasia**
*870 7th Avenue between
West 55th Street and
West 56th Street*

**The rock outcrop
where Edgar Allen
Poe loved to
sit and think**
*Riverside Park near
the intersection of
Riverside Drive and
West 83rd Street*

Marilyn dazzled us here
*Lexington Avenue
between East 51st Street
and East 52nd Street*

**Where Dustin Hoffman
yelled at a cabby,
"Hey! I'm walkin' here!"**
*6th Avenue and
58th Street*

**n Alley: the
e of American
lar music**
*Street, between
and Broadway*

**Audrey Hepburn
had her breakfast
at Tiffany's here**
*Tiffany and Co.,
727 5th Avenue and
East 57th Street*

Here in Manhattan

HERE IN MANHATTAN

A site-by-site guide to the history of the world's greatest city

TOM BEGNAL

SUTHERLAND
HOUSE
TORONTO, 2023

Sutherland House
416 Moore Ave., Suite 205
Toronto, ON M4G 1C9

First edition, Spring 2023

If you are interested in inviting one of our authors to a live event or media appearance, please contact sranasinghe@sutherlandhousebooks.com and visit our website at sutherlandhousebooks.com for more information about our authors and their schedules.

We acknowledge the support of the Government of Canada.

Manufactured in China
Cover designed by Lena Yang
Book composed by Karl Hunt

Library and Archives Canada Cataloguing in Publication
Title: Here in Manhattan : a site-by-site guide to the history
of the world's greatest city / Thomas Begnal.
Names: Begnal, Thomas, author.
Description: Includes index.
Identifiers: Canadiana (print) 20220465967 | Canadiana (ebook) 20220466017 |
ISBN 9781990823084 (hardcover) | ISBN 9781990823169 (EPUB)
Subjects: LCSH: Manhattan (New York, N.Y.)—Guidebooks. | LCSH: Manhattan
(New York, N.Y.)—History, Local. | LCSH: Manhattan (New York, N.Y.)—Anecdotes. |
LCGFT: Guidebooks. | LCGFT: Anecdotes.
Classification: LCC F128.18 .B44 2023 | DDC 917.47/10444—dc23

ISBN 978-1-990823-08-4
eBook 978-1-990823-16-9

To my sister, Mary Joy Begnal

Contents

Introduction

You don't need to be an historian to know that Manhattan and history go together like pastrami and rye. The story of the city is long and rich and wonderfully varied. Indeed, the island has seen it all, from remarkable triumph to horrific tragedy. Not just once, but many times over.

As a result, Manhattan has many individual sites where some remarkable bit of history occurred. Thousands of tourists and working New Yorkers walk past these places every day, blissfully unaware of the great events that happened on the spot. There's a lot to miss if you don't know where to look.

Here in Manhattan: A site-by-site Guide to the History of the World's Greatest City introduces all of those busy tourists and Manhattanites to some of what they are missing. The book features twenty-four stories pulled from the annals of Manhattan's past; some that occurred 250 years ago, others just a few dozen years ago; some that hit the city with the force of an earthquake, others that barely stirred the leaves of a shade tree in Central Park. Each story is interesting enough to warrant a permanent stitch in the permanent fabric of the remarkable island of Manhattan.

The stories are all connected to physical sites that look today very much as they did on the day when history, for better or worse, came along and stamped its mark on the location. Readers can visit these places and have their very own "you are there" moments.

Here in Manhattan is not an exhaustive history of the island but it will leave you with a strong appreciation for the riches encased in the amber of its past. Each of the sites, and the stories behind them, deserve to be kept alive and long remembered. I hope you enjoy them.

Tom Begnal

January, 2023

The Battle of Fort Washington

59 American patriots died here and more than 2,800 were captured when British and Hessian soldiers attacked on November 16, 1776.

Location: Bennett Park – West 183rd Street and Pinehurst Avenue
Nearest subway stop: 181st Street Station/Fort Washington Avenue

....

After George Washington pushed British General William Howe and his 8,000-man army out of Boston on March 17, 1776, the American commander knew that Howe was sure to regroup and attack somewhere in New York City.

New York was important to the colonies because the Hudson River corridor connected to Lake Champlain and ultimately to Canada. If the British could control New York City and the Hudson, they could effectively cut off the New England states from the rest of the colonies. With this in mind, Washington immediately moved troops from Boston to New York and began to reinforce the city.

He built a number of defenses stretching the 13-mile length of Manhattan, from The Battery in the south to the Harlem River in the north. The centerpiece of that effort was a fort in northern Manhattan at the highest point of the island, some 265 feet above sea level. The location overlooked the Hudson River in an area we now call Bennett Park in Washington Heights, although, at the time, the place was mostly wide-open fields and farms populated more by cows, chickens, and pigs than people.

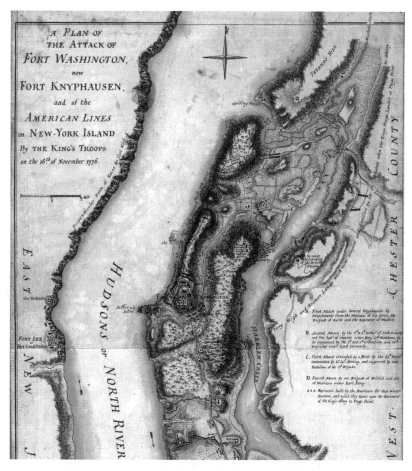

A portion of a map drawn by the British showing the plan of attack on Fort Washington. As shown, the fort is almost directly across the river from Fort Lee, New Jersey and just east of the point on Manhattan's western shore labeled "Jeffery's Hook." Today that location is spelled Jeffrey's Hook and it serves as an anchor point for the east end of the George Washington Bridge. (Map courtesy of Library of Congress, Geography and Map Division)

Under the direction of the chief engineer of the Continental Army, 38-year-old Colonel Rufus Putnam from Massachusetts, troops from Pennsylvania hurriedly constructed the fort during June and July of 1976. Shortly thereafter it was named Fort Washington.

The fort was an irregularly shaped pentagon covering about four acres. It was built to hold about 1,000 men. Some 40 cannon stood at the ready. The outer defenses of the fort extended about one mile to the north and five miles to the south. In total, the Americans had about 2,800 troops; some inside the fort while others were posted to the outer defenses. Commanding the fort was Colonel Robert Magaw, a 38-year-old lawyer raised in Philadelphia and part of the 5th Pennsylvania Battalion.

Not everyone was impressed by the fort. Indeed, one officer, Major Alexander Graton, was very much underwhelmed. In his memoir he wrote

There were no barracks, or casements, or fuel, or water within the body of the place. It was an open earthen construction with ground at a short distance on the back of it equally high, if not higher; without a ditch of any consequence, if there was a ditch at all; no outworks but an incipient one on the north not deserving the appellation, or any of those exterior multiplied obstacles and defenses that, so far as I can judge, could entitle it to the name fortress in any degree capable of sustaining a siege.

In fairness to Putnam, considering the limited time and resources available, it was probably about the best fortification he could put together under such difficult circumstances.

DEDICATION OF FORT WASHINGTON MONUMENT, NEW YORK CITY, NOVEMBER 16, 1901.

On November 16, 1901 – the 125th anniversary of the Battle of Fort Washington – more than one thousand people showed up for the unavailing of a memorial dedicated to those who fought to defend the fort on that day.
(Photo originally published in the book "Fort Washington: An Account of the Identification of the Site of Fort Washington, New York City, and the Erection and Dedication of a Monument thereon Nov. 16, 1901" by The Empire State Society of the American Revolution)

As expected, General Howe did indeed return to New York. After spending time in Halifax, Canada to reorganize, he set sail for New York on June 9th. George Washington, in a letter to his brother John, made it clear he was concerned, saying, "We expect a very bloody summer at New York . . . and I am sorry to say that we are not, either in men or arms, prepared for it."

The first British sails appeared in New York harbor on June 29, 1776. Soon there were 45 warships anchored off Sandy Hook, New Jersey, with many more on the way, including a fleet from England commanded by Admiral Richard Howe, William's older brother.

By August, the armada had swelled to 300 warships and 400 troop transports. Some 32,000 British and Hessian troops were now comfortably encamped on Staten Island. To patriots watching nervously from the shores of Manhattan, it was a frightening display of King George's unmatched land and sea forces. Looking out from The Battery, one American soldier "thought all of London was afloat."

The British went to work on August 22, putting 15,000 troops on shore at Gravesend Bay in Brooklyn. Another 5,000 went ashore a few days later. On the morning of August 27, heralded by a thunderous boom of British cannon fire, the Battle of Long Island was underway. It ended in a crushing defeat for the American army.

Washington then moved his army north, with Howe following. On October 28, the two generals met again in what came to be known as the Battle of White Plains. After heavy fighting and near-equal losses on both sides, Washington withdrew his forces to New Jersey. Howe was now free to focus all his attention on Fort Washington and driving the Continental Army completely out of Manhattan.

As if General Washington's situation was not perilous enough, there was treachery afoot in his fort. On November 2nd, Colonel Magaw's adjutant, William Demont, deserted to the British, slipping unnoticed out of Fort Washington and making his way south to enemy lines. With him were detailed plans he'd made of the entire fort, including the cannon locations. With the plans in his pocket, General Howe now knew every strength and weakness of the main American fort on Manhattan Island. As for William Demont, his treachery likely earned him the infamous distinction as the first traitor to the newly birthed "perfect union."

As General Washington watched from Fort Lee, a mile away across the Hudson River, the British attacked Fort Washington early on November 16th, beginning with a relentless barrage of cannon fire. At about 10 a.m., three British and Hessian divisions went into motion. Lord Hugh Percy led 3,000 British and Hessian forces from the south. General Charles Cornwallis came with an estimated 1,000 British troops from the east, and 4,000 Hessian mercenary troops led by Lieutenant General Wilhelm von Knyphausen pushed down from the north.

About three-quarters of a mile north of the fort was a ridge with an outcropping called Forest Hill in an area known as Long Hill. It was at this outcropping that the Americans met the first wave of von Knyphausen's Hessians with a small contingent of Maryland and Virginia rifleman commanded by 36-year-old Colonel Moses Rawlings from Maryland. The riflemen were supported by a pair of cannons manned by a few members of the first company of Pennsylvanian artillerymen.

Among those artillerymen was John Corbin, a Virginia farmer who joined the Continental Army at the outbreak of the war and was assigned as a matross. The job of a matross was to help the gunners to load and fire the cannons, to move them when necessary and, as they were fired, to regularly sponge the cannon barrels with water to keep them from overheating.

Standing with him on the ridge that day, dressed as a man, was his 25-year-old wife, Margaret Cochran Corbin. While today this might seem inconceivable, during the Revolutionary War it was not unusual for wives to accompany their soldiering husbands. The wives helped by cooking, carrying water, washing and mending clothes, and aiding the sick and wounded.

The fighting on that ridge that day was about as ferocious as it could get. In his 1932 book, *Margaret Corbin, Heroine of the Battle of Fort Washington*, author Edward Hagaman Hall described Knyphausen's attack:

The scene presented at this central point of the height of the battle must have been terrifying even to the stout hearts of the men who defended the hill. A concentrated cannonade from the frigate Pearl on the west, from the 12-pounders and howitzers which Col. Rall stationed on Cock Hill on the north, and from the guns covering the British Landing at 201st Street on the east, filled the air with its thunderous roar, and plunging shot and shell crashing against rocky crags, ploughed the shallow soil and dealt death among the Marylanders and Virginians, while on the rocky slopes swarmed over four thousand mercenary troops, impressive looking in their picturesque uniform of blue coats, yellow breeches, black-top boots, and high-brass mounted caps uttering fierce oaths and charging with bayonetted muskets when firing was impossible.

When one of the gunners was killed, John Corbin quickly stepped in to replace him. It wasn't long before he, too, was struck and

The Fort Washington Monument at Bennett Park as it looks today. The canon that was mounted to the original monument disappeared a few years after the dedication in 1901. The wayside seat that was part of the original design is now also gone. (Photo by author)

killed. At that moment in that place, there was no opportunity for his wife Margaret to mourn his loss. With Hessian bullets and cannonballs and grapeshot filling the air, she immediately took over his job and kept the cannon firing.

Margaret continued at her post until she too was struck and fell, suffering wounds to her arm, chest, and jaw. The patriots held off the onslaught for about two hours before the Hessians overran the position. Later, when the battle ended, the British renamed the outpost Fort Tryon after William Tryon, the Governor of the Province of New York at the time. The area is now part of Fort Tryon Park located just north of 190th Street.

Margaret was captured and became a prisoner of war. She was eventually released, but never fully recovered from her wounds. Three years later the Continental Congress awarded her one-half a soldier's pension.

A plaque honoring her service can be found at Fort Tryon Park near where she was wounded. She died in 1800 and was buried in a paupers' cemetery in Highland Falls, New York, not far from the United States Military Academy at West Point. In 1926, her remains were moved to the Academy grounds and a monument was erected to celebrate her service. It's the only monument at West Point honoring a woman. However, an exhumation of her grave in 2016 showed that the remains belonged to a man, so the search for Margaret is ongoing.

The relentless British attack on Fort Washington continued. Although all the American forces initially offered stiff resistance, their extended lines in several directions were unable to hold the much larger enemy force. Eventually everyone retreated to the fort. By 1 p.m. that day, the entire American force was crammed inside, cheek by jowl. Surrounding them were 8,000 British and Hessian solders.

At 3:00 p.m., faced with certain annihilation, Colonel Magaw surrendered the fort and its 2,800 American troops to the British. An hour later, the American flag was lowered and the British Union flag was raised above the battered fort.

The battle resulted in 59 Americans killed and at least 100 wounded. Hessian losses were 58 killed and about 250 wounded. The British counted 28 killed and more than 100 wounded.

The prisoners were marched to the south end of Manhattan. In his journal, British Lieutenant Frederick Mackenzie described them: "Few of them appeared to have a second shirt, nor did they appear to have washed themselves during the campaign. A great many of them were lads under fifteen and old men, and few had the appearance of soldiers. Their odd figures frequently excited the laughter of our soldiers."

Enlisted men were confined in overcrowded, unheated churches, or old factory buildings, or prison ships anchored in the harbor. Many would soon die from starvation and disease. Indeed, of the 2,800 men taken captive at Fort Washington, 1,100 were dead within four months. The town of Litchfield, Connecticut, had 36 men at Fort Washington. Four died in the fighting and 32 were imprisoned. Of those 32, some 20 died in prison and six died while returning home. Only six survived. The town of Danbury, Connecticut, suffered even more. Of the 50 men from the town who were put in British prisons after the battle, only two came home alive.

Washington and the remainder of the Continental troops retreated to northern New Jersey. It was the lowest point of the war for the Americans. But Washington still had most of his army to work with. They were not done fighting – and better days were on the horizon.

Some 125 years later, on November 16, 1901, the Empire State Society of the Sons of the American Revolution dedicated the Fort Washington Memorial in Bennett Park. The monument is still there, abutting an outcropping of rock that served as the northeastern bastion of the fort.

As part of the dedication, Dr. Peter Brynberg Porter read a poem he had composed for the commemoration. It ended with these two stanzas:

> Enriched with boundless blessings won by those
> Who fought so well in deathless days of yore,
> Well may memorials to their valor here
> Be set by us on Hudson's sacred shore.

> And as the passers-by shall pause, perchance
> To meditate on this historic site,
> From out the memories of that darkest hour
> Will shine "At eventide it will be light."

Tom's Restaurant

Viewers of the TV sitcom *Seinfeld* will recognize it as Monk's Café. It also was the inspiration for the song *Tom's Diner* by singer-songwriter Suzanne Vega. And there's more: it's on the ground floor of an important NASA facility.

Location: 2880 Broadway and West 112th Street
Nearest subway stop: Cathedral Parkway –110th Street Station/Broadway

....

Tom's Restaurant in the Morningside Heights neighborhood of the Upper West Side has been serving up diner food in the same location since Greek immigrant Tom Glikas opened his doors in 1940. He sold the restaurant to relatives in 1946, but the new owners kept the name and, to this day, it's still serving tasty diner food to locals, tourists, and students from nearby Barnard College and Columbia University.

In 1989, a location scout from a California film studio walked into the restaurant and asked Mike Zoulis, one of the owners, if they could photograph the exterior of the place. The scout said the studio needed an outside shot of a restaurant for a new TV series under development. The shot would be used to show the place where the main characters often hung out. Mike signed the release and soon the exterior of Tom's Restaurant would be

The façade of Tom's Restaurant as seen from the angle it was photographed for the *Seinfeld* TV show so that the name "Tom's" was unreadable by viewers. (Photo by author)

seen by millions of viewers each week on a new sitcom called *Seinfeld*.

That shot of Tom's exterior façade was used as the setting for the show's fictional Monk's Café, the place where Jerry Seinfeld and his friends George, Elaine, and Kramer regularly met for a bite to eat. To avoid confusing Tom's and Monk's, the shot was taken at an angle that didn't show "Tom's" in the restaurant name. *Seinfeld* went on to run for nine years and became one of the most popular TV shows of all time.

So how much did the restaurant get paid for signing the release? Not a penny. But Zoulis admits that the Seinfeld connection effectively gave Tom's a mountain of free advertising that has been very good for his business. And, thanks to reruns, he expects

The exterior of Tom's Restaurant as it looks today when viewed from an angle that shows more of the front. (Photo by author)

the agreement to continue paying dividends for many years to come.

The show never did do any actual filming inside Tom's. All the Monk's scenes were done on a sound stage in Los Angeles. That sound stage version of Monk's didn't look at all like the interior of Tom's. However, visitors to Tom's today will find plenty of Seinfeld memorabilia on the walls to remind them of the connection.

Tom's Restaurant also has another distinction. It served as the inspiration for one of Suzanne Vega's most popular songs, *Tom's Diner*. Vega went to school at nearby Barnard College and, later on, while employed as a receptionist downtown, often had morning coffee at Tom's before heading off to work on a southbound subway.

She wrote the song in 1982, well before the place began to enjoy *Seinfeld* fame.

Before going into Tom's, take a moment to look up. The six stories above the restaurant comprise Columbia University's Armstrong Hall, home to NASA's Goddard Institute for Space Studies where a lot of smart people spend each day studying climate change. If you should happen to end up sitting next to one of them at Tom's lunch counter, you just might want to say thanks for the important work they are doing for all of us.

The rock outcrop where Edgar Allan Poe loved to sit and think

He was writing his masterpiece, "The Raven," at the time.

Location: Riverside Park near the intersection of Riverside Drive and West 83rd Street
Nearest subway stop: 79th Street Station/Broadway

....

Edgar Allan Poe was one of America's great nineteenth-century writers. Mainly known for poetry and short stories, he spent a good part of his life as a magazine editor and literary critic, the kind of bread-and-butter work that helped pay the bills when writing fees were few, far-between, and meager, which was most of the time. He also enjoys the distinction of having a team in the National Football League, the Baltimore Ravens, named after his most famous poem.

I was introduced to Edgar Allan Poe in junior high. For me, back then, a typical homework reading assignment for English class was rarely something to be enjoyed but rather a task to be dutifully endured. A good many of the stories didn't ring my interest bell. However, every now and then the assignment would sound a loud and clear note. Such was the case when the author assigned was Edgar Allan Poe.

His writing was wonderfully different. Most other assigned stories were non-carbonated. But Poe's had zip. And fizz. And bite. A Poe story was an ice-cold fountain Coca-Cola with a shot of cherry syrup stirred in. Almost always there was the suggestion of fear – sometimes a little, sometimes a lot – but never so much that I had to hide under the bed covers at night. His work has been variously described as dark, gothic, macabre, mysterious, and supernatural. For me, however, Edgar Allan Poe was just plain fun to read.

Apparently, my dim junior high school brain was onto something. The British author Arthur Conan Doyle, of Sherlock Holmes fame, said of Poe: "In him American literature is anchored,

Mount Tom in Riverside Park, a place overlooking the Hudson River, where Poe often sat to enjoy the solitude while he was writing The Raven at the nearby Brennan house. (Photo by author)

in him alone, on solid ground." Another Brit, George Bernard Shaw, observed that "Poe constantly and inevitably produced magic where his greatest contemporaries produced only beauty." Allan Ginsberg, the Beat Generation poet of the 1950s, argued, "Everything leads to Poe. You can trace all literary art to Poe's influence: Burroughs, Baudelaire, Genet, Dylan . . . It all leads back to Poe." And, in an interview, movie director Alfred Hitchcock revealed "It's because I liked Edgar Allan Poe's stories so much that I began to make suspense films."

The family history on Poe's father's side can be traced to Northern Ireland. His great-grandparents, John Poe and Jane McBride Poe, immigrated to America from there; John arriving around the year 1745, and Jane, who would later become his wife, showing up closer to 1749.

Their son, David Poe, Edgar's grandfather, served with distinction during the Revolutionary War to the extent that Marquis de Lafayette, on his final visit to America after the war, went to the old soldier's grave in Baltimore and declared while kissing the ground, "Ici repose un coeur noble" (Here rests a noble heart).

Edgar was born in the city of Boston in 1809, the second of three children, to David, Jr. and Elizabeth Poe. Both of his parents were actors. In the year 1811, when the family was living and working in Richmond, Virginia, his father packed up and bolted from the house for good. He died a few months later. Just a few days after his passing, Elizabeth died after suffering from what most likely was tuberculosis, a disease known at the time as consumption.

The three orphaned children were taken in by different families. Edgar went to the home of John and Frances Allan, a childless

Poe at about 30 years of age.
(Edgar Allan Poe Memorial
Association, Wikimedia Commons)

Richmond couple. John was in the tobacco business. He was not wealthy but apparently had enough money to make sure Edgar was enrolled in a good private school. The couple never adopted Edgar, but they did impart "Allan" to him as a middle name.

In 1815, John Allan sailed to England for an extended visit in hopes of expanding his business, bringing along his wife, her younger sister, and Edgar. They ended up staying five years, and Edgar spent most of that time at boarding school.

Returning to Richmond in 1820, Edgar continued his education at the school of Joseph H. Clarke. Years later, Clarke would recount, "Edgar Poe was five years in my school. During that time he read Ovid, Caesar, Virgil, Cicero, and Horace in Latin, and Xenophon and Homer in Greek. He showed a much stronger taste for classic poetry than he did for classic prose. He had no love for mathematics, but his poetical compositions were universally admitted to be the best in the school. While the other boys wrote mere mechanical verses, Poe wrote genuine poetry: the boy was a born poet."

Edgar began attending the University of Virginia in 1826. That same year he also became engaged to Sarah Elmira Royster, a childhood neighbor one year his junior. Unfortunately for the pair, Sarah's father insisted they were too young for marriage. He scuppered the romance by intercepting and destroying Poe's letters to her. Assuming Edgar had lost interest in their relationship, Sarah ended the engagement. About two years later she became Sarah Elmira Royster Shelton when she married Alexander Shelton, a successful and wealthy businessman from Richmond.

Despite his disappointment at losing Sarah, Edgar still managed to excel academically at the University of Virginia. However, John Poe was tight-fisted when it came to providing Edgar with enough money to support himself at school. Edgar turned to gambling to try and make up the shortage, but that only made things worse. He also began to drink. One classmate recalled:

> He would always seize the tempting glass, generally unmixed with sugar or water – in fact, perfectly straight – and without the least apparent pleasure, swallow the contents, never pausing until the last drop had passed his lips. One glass at a time was all that he could take; but this was sufficient to rouse his whole nervous nature into a state of strongest excitement, which found vent in a continuous flow of wild, fascinating talk that irresistibly enchanted every listener with siren-like power.

The bottle would torment him for the rest of his life. Meanwhile, his gambling debts ended up causing a falling out between Edgar and his stepfather. John cut off his income entirely and Edgar had to leave school after just one year. Poe was now on his own. He enlisted for five-years in the U.S. Army's First Regiment of Artillery, spending most of that period at three locations: Fort Independence on Castle Island in Boston, Fort Moultrie on Sullivan's Island in South Carolina, and Fort Monroe in Hampton, Virginia. While still serving, in 1827, he paid to print 50 copies of his poetic works, titled "Tamerlane and Other Poems." It was his first published work.

It took only two years for Poe to earn the rank of First Sargent of Artillery, the highest achievable rank as an enlisted man. He then secured an early discharge to enroll in the United States Military Academy and the year 1830 found him at West Point. Poe did well academically, but the rigid, controlled routine of the school proved to be unbearable and he wanted out. After less than a year at the Academy, he got himself court-martialed and expelled by repeatedly skipping roll calls, classes, parades, guard duty, and chapel.

In 1832, a Baltimore newspaper ran a writing contest in which Poe won first place and $50 for his short story *MS Found in a Bottle*. It was the earliest recognition of his talent. Shortly after winning, he stopped by the office of one of the judges, John H.B. Latrobe, to thank him. Years later, Latrobe recalled the visit:

> He was, if anything, below the middle size, and yet could not be described as a small man. His figure was remarkably good, and he carried himself erect and well, as one who had been trained to it. He was dressed in black and his frock coat was buttoned to the

21

Poe at 39 years of age, about a year before his death. Photo of daguerreotype by W.S. Hartshorn, 1848. (C.T. Tatman, circa 1904. Library of Congress, Prints & Photograph Division)

throat where it met the black stock, then almost universally worn. Not a particle of white was visible. Coat, hat, boots, and gloves had very evidently seen their best days, but so far as brushing and mending could go, everything had been done, apparently, to make them presentable. Gentleman was written all over him. His manner was easy and quiet. The expression of his face was grave, almost sad, except when he was engaged in conversation, when it became animated and changeable. His voice, I remember, was very pleasing in its tone, and well-modulate, almost mythical and his words were well chosen and unhesitating.

In 1835, Poe was working as an editor, writer, and critic for the Southern Literary Messenger magazine in Richmond, Va. In September of that year, while in Baltimore and with the blessing of his aunt Maria Poe Clemm (his father's sister), Poe eloped with her 13-year-old daughter, Virginia Elizabeth Clemm. The couple made the marriage public with a wedding held in Richmond on May 16, 1836.

Poe first met Virginia in 1830 in Baltimore when he moved in with her family shortly after he got out of the army. She was seven-years old and living with her mother Maria Poe Clemm, her brother Henry, and her grandmother, Elizabeth Carnes Poe. While living there, Poe met Mary Devereaux, a neighbor and was soon enamored by her. How long that relationship lasted isn't clear. It's also not clear when Poe began to have romantic feelings for Virginia, but we know he began thinking about marrying her in 1835 while he was at the Southern Literary Messenger.

His deep love for her is expressed in several of his poems, most famously, *Anabelle Lee*. She devoted her life to him.

In 1838, Poe wrote his only novel, *The Narrative of Arthur Gordon Pym*. In 1839 he moved his family to Philadelphia and took a job for $10 a week as an assistant editor for *Burton's Gentleman's Magazine*.

Poe much preferred to write poetry, but short stories were more marketable, so he wrote several during that period. They included some of his best work, including *The Fall of the House of Usher* (1839), *The Murders in the Rue Morgue* (1841), *The Pit and the Pendulum* (1842), *The Tell-Tale Heart* (1843), *The Black Cat* (1843), *The Gold Bug* (1843), and *The Cask of Amontillado* (1846).

In 1844, after moving to New York, Poe rented the second floor of a two-story farmhouse owned by Patrick Brennan and his wife Mary. Virginia and her mother joined him. The house sat on

The Brennan house in northern Manhattan where Poe lived while writing The Raven. (Steel engraving by S. Hollyer. Library of Congress, Prints & Photograph Division)

216 acres of rolling countryside in northern Manhattan, where it was hoped the fresh country air would aid Virginia's recovery from tuberculosis. If it hadn't been torn down in 1888, the house would be found today on what is now West 84th Street between Broadway and Amsterdam Avenue.

While there, Poe would often walk a short distance to a rocky outcropping that offered a wonderful view of the Hudson River. Mary Brennan noted that "It was Poe's custom to wander away from the house in pleasant weather to 'Mount Tom,' an immense rock which may still be seen in Riverside Park, where he would sit alone for hours, gazing at the Hudson."

During his time at the Brennan farmhouse, Poe completed his masterpiece poem, "The Raven." It was published in 1845, and, for his effort, Poe was paid about $20. Although the poem earned him little money, it did win him instant national fame. Newspapers from coast-to-coast printed "The Raven" and it was wildly popular.

In light of his new found success, Poe felt it important to be closer to where the publishing action was, so he and Virginia and his mother-in-law moved to lower Manhattan. However, within 18 months or so, Virginia's health was again a concern and the family moved once more to "the country," this time to the northern wilds of Fordham Village, part of what is now Fordham University in the Bronx. The house still stands today and is open to the public as a museum.

In 1846, Mrs. Mary Gove Nichols visited the Poes in Fordham and recorded this description of Virginia and her mother:

On this occasion I was introduced to the young wife of the poet, and to the mother, then more than sixty years of age. She was

The Brennan house in 1879 as seen after the land adjacent to it had been excavated, graded, and leveled when the city began introducing a grid system of streets that would forever change the face of Manhattan. The house was torn down in 1888. (New York Historical Society)

a tall, dignified old lady, with a most ladylike manner, and her black dress, though old and much worn, looked really elegant on her. She wore a widow's cap of the genuine pattern, and it suited exquisitely with her snow-white hair. Her features were large, and corresponded with her stature, and it seemed strange how such a stalwart and queenly woman could be the mother of her almost petite daughter. Mrs. Poe looked very young; she had large black eyes, and a pearly whiteness of complexion, which was a perfect pallor. Her pale face, her brilliant eyes, and her raven hair gave her an unearthly look. One felt that she was almost a disrobed spirit, and when she coughed it was made certain that she was rapidly passing away.

Mrs. Nichols added to her story later that year:

The autumn came, and Mrs. Poe sank rapidly in consumption, and I saw her in her bed chamber. Everything here was so neat, so purely clean, so scant and poverty-stricken, that I saw the sufferer with such a heartache as the poor feel for the poor. There was no clothing on the bed, which was only straw, but a snow-white spread and sheets. The weather was cold, and the sick lady had the dreadful chills that accompany the hectic fever of consumption. She lay on the straw bed, wrapped in her husband's great-coat, with a large tortoise-shell cat on her bosom. The wonderful cat seemed conscious of her great usefulness. The coat and the cat were the sufferer's only means of warmth, except as her husband held her hands, and her mother her feet.

Seeing firsthand the struggles facing the family, she returned to New York and set about getting them some relief. She soon collected from her network of friends "a featherbed and abundance of bed-clothing and other comforts" and $60 in cash. Nevertheless, Virginia's health continued to worsen and she died on January 30, 1847. She was 24 years old.

In 1848, Poe wrote in a letter:

Six years ago, a wife, whom I loved as no man ever loved before, ruptured a blood-vessel in singing. Her life was despaired of. I took leave of her forever and underwent all the agonies of her death. She recovered partially and I again hoped. At the end of a year the vessel broke again – I went through precisely the same scene. Again in about a year afterward. Then again – again – again and even once again at varying intervals. Each time I felt all the agonies of her death – and at each accession of the disorder I loved her more dearly and clung to her life with more desperate pertinacity. But I am constitutionally sensitive – nervous in a very unusual degree. I became insane, with long intervals of horrible sanity. During these fits of absolute unconsciousness I drank, God only knows how often or how much. As a matter of course, my enemies referred the insanity to the drink rather than the drink to the insanity. I had indeed, nearly abandoned all hope of a permanent cure when I found one in the death of my wife. This I can and do endure as becomes a man – it was the horrible never-ending oscillation between hope and despair which I could not longer have endured without the total loss of reason. In the death of what was my life, then, I receive a new but – oh God! how melancholy an existence.

As the year 1848 reached a close, Poe found himself becoming enamored of the poet Sarah Helen Whitman of Providence, Rhode Island, and soon proposed marriage.

Sarah was intrigued but also well aware of his drinking issues. By now Poe was also taking laudanum, a potent concoction made from a mix of opium and alcohol. Whitman ended the relationship when it became clear that she would not cure him of either habit.

Despite the romantic disappointment, Poe continued to forge ahead. He had long dreamed of owning a literary magazine, planning to call it *The Stylus*, and he now set about in earnest to raise cash for the enterprise by scheduling a lecture tour throughout several southern states.

While in Richmond, Poe made an unannounced visit to the old flame of his youth, Sarah Elmira Royster Shelton, who had been widowed five years earlier. Poe soon proposed marriage to her, but Sarah was hesitant. He was drinking too much. Plus, her family was strongly opposed to the idea. And, perhaps the biggest kicker: she had inherited $100,000 from her husband upon his death, but his will stated she would lose a good part of it if she ever remarried. Despite all her concerns, it is generally believed she agreed to marriage, although not all Poe historians are certain that it came to pass. However, we do know that at about the same time, Poe began a serious effort to stop drinking by joining the local chapter of the Sons of Temperance, an organization dedicated to getting its members sober.

On September 27, 1849, Poe boarded a steamship in Richmond and headed for New York, intending to collect his beloved mother-in-law, Maria Clemm, and bring her back to Richmond for the wedding. The next day the ship made a scheduled stop in Baltimore.

What happened over the next several days remains unclear, but we know that Poe was found on October 3rd on a Baltimore street, in the rain, semi-conscious, unable to move, and dressed in shabby clothes that clearly didn't belong to him. He was immediately brought to Washington College University Hospital and put under the care of Dr. John J. Moran. Poe died four days later, at the age of 40. While in hospital he had not been able to explain exactly what happened to him on that Baltimore street. His last words, according to Dr. Moran, were "Lord, help my poor soul."

Dr. Moran concluded that Poe's death was the result of being beaten during a robbery. He also insisted there was no evidence that Poe had been drinking. But others have suggested a variety of other causes of death, including flu, rabies, syphilis, hypoglycemia, pneumonia, cholera, and brain tumor.

Because he was found outside a voting place on an election day, it was also believed he might have been subjected to an illegal practice called cooping. Hired goons would pressure victims, usually after plying them with alcohol, to vote for a particular candidate not just once but several times. To avoid being detected, the victims would be put into a new change of clothes between each visit to the ballot box.

Poe was buried in Baltimore at the Westminster Hall and Burying Ground in a plot of ground owned by his grandfather. Only a handful of mourners showed up. Some 26 years later, in 1875, his remains were moved to another location at the cemetery that included a new and large monument. His wife Virginia and mother-in-law Maria Clemm are buried nearby. Over a thousand people, including the poet Walt Whitman, showed up for the formal dedication of the monument.

Mount Tom is located in Riverside Park between the western ends of West 83rd Street and West 84th Street. Several paths lead to the rock outcropping. I'd suggest finding the highest point on the rock as Poe would likely have done the same. Once there, sit for a spell and, as the poet did some 180 years ago, enjoy the surrounding view. You never know what it might inspire.

The first pedestrian death caused by an automobile in the United States happened here

The victim was struck while exiting a trolley.

Location: Central Park West and 74th Street
Nearest subway stop: 72nd Street Station/Central Park West

....

Fame can strike anyone at any time for just about any reason – but that's not to say that it's always welcome.

At about 10 p.m. on Wednesday, September 13, 1899, Henry Hale Bliss was riding a southbound 8th Avenue electric trolley car in Manhattan. Bliss, a 69-year-old real estate broker, was heading home to his residence at 235 West 75th Street.

The trolley made its regular stop at the intersection of West 74th Street and Central Park West, and, as Bliss stepped off, he turned to offer a hand to a female acquaintance. In that brief moment of distraction, he was knocked down and run over by a northbound electric cab operated by the Electric Vehicle Company. His head and chest were crushed, and he died the next morning at Roosevelt Hospital.

Thus, Mr. Bliss earned himself a place in history as the first pedestrian in the United States to be killed by an automobile. The news of the event had legs long enough to carry the story all the

It was a circa 1900 electric cab – perhaps one like these two seen here passing in front of the old Metropolitan Opera House on 39th Street – that struck and killed Henry Hale Bliss. The carriage design was based on the horse-drawn hansom cabs that were in common use at the time. (Wikimedia Commons, photographer unknown)

way to Illinois, where the Alton *Evening Telegraph* grimly stated, "The automobile has tasted blood." It was not easily sated. Indeed, according to the Federal Highway Administration, over the next century automobiles killed more than 700,000 pedestrians in the United States. That's more than the number of Americans who died in every war since the Civil War.

The driver of the cab, Arthur Smith, was immediately arrested and charged with manslaughter. He explained to police that he had to steer close to the trolley in order to go around a large truck parked on the right side of Central Park West. The charges were later dropped after it was concluded the death of Bliss was unintentional.

The lone passenger in Smith's cab was Dr. David Orr Edson, the son of Franklin Edson, the former New York City mayor who served from 1883 to 1884. Dr. Edson was returning from a house

Part of an illustration accompanying an article titled "The 'Death Stretch' Beside the Park" published in the September 15, 1899 issue of the New York Journal and Advertiser. It shows the traffic and pedestrian congestion that was common to the area where Henry Hale Bliss was killed and lists a number of serious trolly-related accidents that occurred there over a period of just a few months in 1899.

The intersection of Central Park West and 74th Street as it looks today. (Photo by author)

call in Harlem. He quickly summoned an ambulance and, as best he could, attended to Mr. Bliss before the badly injured man was taken to the hospital.

On September 13, 1999, the centenary of Bliss's accident, a ceremony was held at the site to raise awareness of pedestrian safety. As part of the program, a commemorative plaque was installed at the intersection. The great-granddaughter of Henry Hale Bliss placed pink and red roses on the spot where he was struck down.

Should present-day visitors decide to cross the street while visiting the intersection, using the pedestrian crossing-light signal is strongly recommended. As always, don't forget to look both ways before stepping out.

A plaque mounted to a traffic-light pole marks the intersection where Henry Hale Bliss meet his fate. (Photo by author)

Where Dustin Hoffman yelled at a cabby, "Hey! I'm walkin' here!"

It's the location of an iconic scene from the Academy Award–winning movie *Midnight Cowboy*.

Location: 6th Avenue and 58th Street
Nearest subway stop: 57th Street Station/6th Avenue

....

Despite being assigned an X-rating on its release on May 25, 1969, *Midnight Cowboy* quickly became a critical and financial success – much to the surprise of many in the film industry. The movie received seven Oscar nominations and three awards, including best picture. It also raked in almost $45 million at the box office. Not bad for a movie made for about $3.6 million.

The two main characters are Ratso Rizzo and Joe Buck. Ratso is a streetwise but sickly, down-on-his luck, Manhattan con-man played by Dustin Hoffman in his first film since his 1967 breakout roll as Benjamin Braddock, the socially flummoxed college graduate in the blockbuster *The Graduate*. Joe Buck, played by newcomer Jon Voight, is a babe-in-the-woods Texan, newly arrived in Manhattan with grand plans to earn his fortune as a male prostitute. To get the role, Voight worked "for scale," the movie industry term for minimum wage. Both actors went on to enjoy stellar careers in Hollywood.

Ratso Rizzo (played by Dustin Hoffman) explains to a cabbie exactly who is walking where. Joe Buck (played by John Voight) looks on. (Courtesy of MGM Media Licensing)

In a classic scene, Ratso and Joe walk side-by-side heading north on the east side of a very busy 6th Avenue in Manhattan. Ratso, shuffling along with his noticeably gimpy leg, is doing all the talking.

We already know that both men have little to show for themselves. Yet, somehow, the two manage to keep a tight grip on dreams promising better days ahead. Ratso wants nothing more than to scrounge up just enough cash to get himself down to the sunshine and warmth of Florida. Joe wants to live the highlife as the top gigolo in Manhattan.

As they step out onto 58th Street, a speeding yellow cab trying to beat a red light screeches to a stop just inches from Rizzo. Without missing a beat, as his cigarette falls from his open mouth, he turns and pounds his left hand on the hood of the cab while screaming at the driver, "Hey! I'm walkin' here! I'm walkin' here!"

Rizzo and the cabby exchange a few more heated words and hand gestures before the cab quickly drives off. Rizzo and Buck continue walking and talking, almost as though nothing ever happened.

It has long been unclear whether or not the sudden appearance of the cab at the intersection was serendipitous or planned by the filmmakers. Director John Schlesinger said, "I don't know that that was improvised. I think we got an extra inside a cab and did it. I can't swear to the fact that it was in the script or not, but I don't think that was improvised." Producer Jerome Hellman said he remembers the scene filmed with an extra in the cab.

The script as originally written by screenwriter Waldo Salt does indeed include an encounter with a cab at the intersection, but it's not exactly what ended up on film. Salt described the walk down 6th Avenue by Ratso and Joe like this:

RATSO

"Look, with these chicks that want to buy it, most of 'em are older, dignified, right? Social register types. They can't be trotting down to Times Square to pick out the merchandise. They need a middleman, right? That's O'Daniel."

Joe hesitates as Ratso darts into traffic against a red light, yelling unheard obscenities at a cab driver who blasts his horn. Joe runs recklessly forward as Ratso slams the taxi fender with his fist, pretending to be hit, falling into Joe's arms. The taxi stops, halting traffic. Ratso recovers, strolls casually in front of the cab, biting his thumb at the driver.

RATSO (CONT'D)

"It is a crime, a stud like you passing out double sawbucks to a chick like that. With proper management you should be taking home fifty, a hundred bucks a day. More if you wanta moonlight."

Interestingly, in a 2012 interview with Canada's *National Post*, Dustin Hoffman seemed to suggest that a cab was not supposed to be in the scene at all when they were filming that day.

Hoffman said the plan was simply to have the two actors time their walk so that the traffic light on 6th Avenue would turn green just as they reached the intersection. That way they could continue to walk while legally crossing the street and not miss a beat. If they didn't time it right, they'd have to stop walking at the edge of the sidewalk and continue with their dialog while standing there waiting for the light to change; but director Schlesinger didn't want any standing in this scene, only walking and talking.

Hoffman went on to say that it took a number of takes to get the timing right. When they finally reached the edge of the sidewalk at just the right moment, a cabby came along out of the blue thinking he could beat the light. The cab had to screech to a halt when Hoffman and Voight stepped off the sidewalk. That's when Hoffman turned to face the cabby and explained to him exactly who it was that was walking there. And a new catch-phrase was added to our lexicon.

The suggestion by Hoffman that the appearance of the cab was unplanned has some merit. The filmmakers didn't get a permit to close down the street for the shoot, probably to save a few bucks. A permit costs money, as does the required insurance that goes with it. Then, too, they'd have to get a bunch of extras to fill the sidewalk and spend time telling them what to do (and, of course, pay them).

Instead, they gambled on not getting caught and fined and simply put the two actors on the crowded sidewalk filled with anonymous New Yorkers going about their daily lives. Then they

The intersection as it looks today viewed from the east side of the Ritz-Carlton hotel on 6th Avenue. (Photo by author)

equipped Hoffman and Buck with remote microphones and shot the scene with a camera set up in a van parked across the street. The industry calls this "guerrilla-style" filmmaking.

So, Hoffman's story makes sense – a random cabby in a hurry trying to beat a light on 58th Street nearly hit the film star as he started crossing the street while shooting a scene for a movie that didn't have a permit to shut down the street. And, at that moment, unrehearsed, Hoffman improvised his lines to give the cabby a full dose of New York cheer.

Schlesinger, who filmed the chance near-death encounter, apparently loved what he saw. Nevertheless, he felt the scene could be improved with a bit more work. Reportedly, he arranged to hire someone to drive a cab and recreate the scene. It required several more takes, but Schlesinger finally got what he wanted. As a result, the scene you see in the movie is staged, but it's based on an earlier close encounter by Hoffman with a real cabby who was in a real hurry.

You can recapture the movie-camera view by standing on the east side of 6th Ave. just north of 58th Street. That puts you next to the Ritz-Carlton Hotel building along 6th Avenue. Look south to the east side of 6th Ave and you'll recognize the spot where Ratso and Joe crossed 58th Street. You won't see those two walking together along 6th Avenue. However, you will almost certainly see a good many people who, like them, continue to hold tight onto dreams that promise better days just ahead.

Audrey Hepburn had her breakfast at Tiffany's here

She window-shops at the famous jewelry store while enjoying a Danish pastry and a cup of to-go coffee.

Location: Tiffany and Co., 727 5th Avenue and East 57th Street
Nearest subway stop: 5th Avenue Station/59th Street

....

The early morning sun is just starting to slip through the canyons of Manhattan as a yellow taxi drops off a passenger in front of a stately Art Deco building on a deserted 5th Avenue. The passenger – a tall, thin, dark-haired, and strikingly beautiful woman – wears an elegant black dress and carries with her a white scarf, black purse, and small paper bag. A pair of oversized sunglasses rest on her slightly upturned nose.

Looking up, she sees the words "Tiffany & Co." engraved in the façade over the doorway. Above the engraving is a circular clock resting on the shoulders of a nine-foot statue of Atlas, the famous Titan from Greek mythology. While the full face of the clock never quite makes it into the entire camera frame, the little hand is clearly on the number six, giving us a clue as to the hour.

Approaching the nearest window, the woman delicately opens the bag and takes out a pastry and a coffee in a paper cup before gazing up at the sparkling display behind the glass.

Audrey Hepburn (as Holly Golightly) looks at one of Tiffany's window displays while having a quick breakfast – a cup of to-go coffee in a paper cup and a sweet pastry. (screenshot of movie trailer, Wikimedia Commons)

It's the opening scene from the movie *Breakfast at Tiffany's*. As the credits roll, we get our first glimpse of Audrey Hepburn playing the iconic character of Holiday (Holly) Golightly wearing an iconic dress for this iconic scene in an iconic movie while standing in front of an iconic jewelry store as *Moon River*, the iconic song by Johnny Mercer and Henry Mancini, plays in the background. That's a lot of iconic entertainment packed into about 2 minutes and 30 seconds.

The movie, loosely based on the Truman Capote novella of the same name, debuted in theaters across the United States in October 1961. Written by screenwriter George Axelrod and directed by Blake Edwards, it reportedly cost Paramount Studios about $2.5 million to make and generated $15 million or so in box office sales. Her role as Holly Golightly earned Hepburn an Academy Award nomination for best actress. Axelrod was nominated for best adapted screenplay, while Mercer and Mancini won Oscars for *Moon River*.

Later in the movie, when talking to her love interest Paul Varjak (played by co-star George Peppard), we find out why Holly was at Tiffany's that morning.

Holly
"You know those days when you get the mean reds?"

Paul
"The mean reds, you mean like the blues?"

Holly
"No. The blues are because you're getting fat and maybe it's been raining too long; you're just sad, that's all. The mean reds are horrible. Suddenly you're afraid and you don't know what you're afraid of. Do you ever get that feeling? . . . Well, when I get it the only thing that does any good is to jump in a cab and go to Tiffany's. Calms me down right away. The quietness and the proud look of it. Nothing very bad could happen to you there. If I could find a real-life place that'd make me feel like Tiffany's, then – then I'd buy some furniture and give the cat a name!"

What Holly calls the "mean reds" would likely today be understood as a bout of depression of some sort. To know that a visit to Tiffany's helps boost her spirits – even if only for a short time – is to gain an understanding of Holly that becomes clearer later when we learn she makes her living as an "escort." Exactly what that means in the film is left intentionally vague.

That Holly was drawn to Tiffany's window would probably not have surprised long time employee Gene Moore. For almost 40 years, starting in 1955, Moore was Tiffany's window dresser. During that time period he created more than 5,000 window displays for the store and turned the work into an art form. "When someone looks into a Tiffany window," he said, "I want him or her to do a double – even a triple – take. I want him to experience the sudden fresh insight the Zen philosophers call the 'ahness' of things." Perhaps that 'ahness' was part of Tiffany's appeal to Holly.

The role of Holly Golightly didn't fall automatically to Hepburn. Edwards first offered it to Shirley MacLaine, but she turned it down. That decision, MacLaine would later admit, was one of her biggest regrets. But she also said at the time, most graciously, "Never would I have given Holly Golightly what Audrey did."

Early on, when the film was being cast, Truman Capote lobbied hard for Marilyn Monroe to play Holly. He felt she would be better able to embody the character of Holly as she appears in the book. But Axelrod's screenplay softened some of the rougher edges of her character and Blake Edwards felt Hepburn was better suited to the movie version of Holly.

The black dress she wears in the opening scene was designed by French fashion designer Hubert de Givenchy. He was at the top of his game at the time, with clients that included Lauren Bacall, Ingrid Bergman, Maria Callas, Marlene Dietrich, Greta Garbo, Grace Kelly, Sophia Loren, and Jacqueline Kennedy. After Audrey Hepburn died in 1993, Givenchy donated the dress to City of Joy Aid, a charity dedicated to improving living conditions for the most underprivileged in India. In 2006, the dress was auctioned off at

Christie's for more than $900,000. The money was used to buy a school for the poor in Kolkata.

When Hepburn's two sons put about 250 items from her personal collection up for auction in 2017, Tiffany & Co. bid almost $850,000 for her original 140-page working script of the movie. That she took her craft seriously is obvious from the many handwritten notes in the margins throughout. The script is now in Tiffany's archive.

Before you finish window shopping at Tiffany's, take a moment to look above the entrance and admire that statue of Atlas, a figure that has been welcoming shoppers to the store for over 165 years. It was carved out of wood by Henry Frederick Metzler, a friend of founder Charles Lewis Tiffany. Painted to look like weathered bronze, the statue was installed above the door of Tiffany's store at 550 Broadway when it opened in 1853. In 1870, when Tiffany's moved to Union Square and 15th Avenue, the statue went with it. Then, in 1905, it came along when Tiffany's moved to 5th Avenue and 37th Street. The well-traveled statue has been at its current home, 727 5th Avenue, since the store opened there in 1940.

That Atlas statue has no doubt observed millions of Tiffany window shoppers over the years. If the old Titan could talk, he'd be hard-pressed to recall anyone with more style, grace, and elegance than Audrey Hepburn when, in 1961, she arrived as Holly Golightly in that early morning cab, hoping for a few moments to chase away those horrible mean reds.

Where a hail of hot lead cut down mob boss Albert Anastasia

Two gunmen entered the barber shop at the Park Central Hotel and shot dead the head of the Anastasia crime family as he sat to get a haircut.

Location: 870 7th Avenue between West 55th Street and West 56th Street
Nearest subway stop: 57th Street Station/7th Avenue

....

It was about 10:15 a.m. on Friday, October 25, 1957, when 55-year-old Albert Anastasia walked through a busy corridor connected to the lobby of the Park Sheraton Hotel (now the Park Central Hotel) and into Arthur Grasso's barber shop looking to get a haircut. It was a routine he'd followed many times over the years. In addition to Grasso and Anastasia, 11 people were in the shop – five barbers, two customers, two shoe-shiners, a valet, and a manicurist. Anastasia's bodyguard was parking the car.

As usual, the 65-year-old owner of the shop greeted Anastasia at the door. There were 10 barber chairs in the shop and Anastasia headed over to barber Joseph Bocchino who settled him comfortably into chair number 4, one of four chairs along a mirrored wall on the West 55th Street side of the shop. No sooner had Bocchino started cutting than two men drawing guns walked into the shop. Both wore fedoras, dark suits, dark green sunglasses, and had their faces partially covered with scarves.

Anastasia sprang from the chair just as the men pushed aside the barber. The armed duo fired off ten shots in a matter of seconds. Five found their mark, one of them to the back of Anastasia's head. Anastasia fell to the floor, motionless. In all likelihood, he was already dead. The gunmen casually walked out the door and into a waiting getaway car in which they quickly disappeared down the street. The two were never caught.

So ended the life of one America's most powerful organized crime figures. He had been a notorious member of Murder, Inc., the murder-for-hire organization that was believed to be responsible for dozens of mob executions in the 1930s and 1940s. If a mobster needed someone rubbed out, and if the hit was approved by the higher-ups, Murder, Inc. would get it done for the right fee. Anastasia's nickname had been "Lord High Executioner."

Born Umberto Anastasio in Calabria, Italy, on February 26, 1902, he was the oldest of 12 children. At 17, he and brothers Anthony and Joseph got jobs as deckhands on an ocean freighter. In 1919, while in New York harbor, the three jumped ship and found jobs on the local docks.

A mug shot of 34-year-old Anastasia taken by the New York City police in 1936. (Photo from Wikimedia Commons)

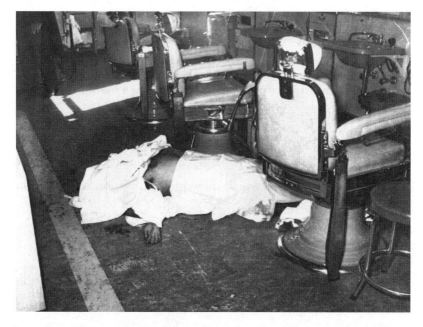

The body of Albert Anastasia lies on the floor of Arthur Grasso's barber shop after two gunmen barged in and shot him several times as he sat to get a haircut. (Everett Collection/Alamy Stock Photo)

It didn't take long for Anastasia to get into trouble. In 1921, when he was just 19, he and a ne'er-do-well associate were convicted of killing a fellow dock worker. Both men received the death penalty and were sent to Sing Sing Prison in Ossining, New York, to await a visit to the electric chair. It was around this time that he Americanized his first name to Albert and changed his last name to Anastasia in order to avoid disgracing the family name.

However, after 18 months on death row, the Court of Appeals reversed the verdict on a technicality and ordered a new trial. By the time it was set to start, four of the main witnesses against Anastasia had either disappeared or been killed. Anastasia was acquitted.

The barber shop where Albert Anastasia met his fate is now a coffee house. (Photo by author)

Throughout his life, Anastasia and trouble were as conjoined as pasta and red sauce. By 1936, he had been arrested nine times, five for homicide. Remarkably, he spent little time in prison: he got two years after being convicted in 1923 for carrying a concealed weapon, and in 1955, he served a year in federal prison for failing to pay $12,000 owed in income tax.

Visit the Park Central Hotel today and you won't find a barber shop. What was once Arthur Grasso's place is now a Starbucks with an entrance on 7th Avenue. There is no longer any direct access from there to the hotel. But, if you go inside for a latte, you'll indeed be standing in the same room where the "Lord High Executioner" was himself ingloriously executed on that late October day in 1957.

The disco where the world's beautiful people danced the night away

Everyone who was anyone had to be seen there.

Location: 254 West 54th Street, between 8th Avenue and Broadway
Nearest subway stop: 7th Avenue Station/West 53rd Street

....

Studio 54 was a nightclub like none before. Launched in the spring of 1977, its popularity instantly soared into the stratosphere, lighting up Manhattan with the candlepower of a rocket ship bound for entertainment immortality. Less than three years later, it all came crashing down. Yet for the short time it blazed in the night sky above 54th Street, the place burned white hot, fueled by a mix of celebrity, music, dancing, stagecraft and, oftentimes, a generous measure of sex and drugs.

The big music trend at the time was disco, and it blasted across the crowded dance floor at Studio 54 with the energy of a nuclear reactor. Celebrities loved the place. A-list actors, artists, writers, models, musicians, filmmakers, fashion designers, athletes, and business tycoons showed up to dance and smile and wave to the paparazzi. Joining them were those folks who hoped someday to be an A-Lister or, at the very least, rub elbows with them. Everyone there, however, had one thing in common – they loved disco and they loved to dance.

Studio 54 was the brainchild of 33-year-old Steve Rubell and 30-year-old Ian Schrager, two entrepreneurial Brooklynites who met as fraternity brothers in the 1960s at Syracuse University. They started out owning a few steakhouses before opening up a couple of smallish nightclubs, one in Boston and one in New Haven.

In 1975, they opened a nightclub in Douglaston, Queens, at an old 11-room stone mansion that had seen time as a clubhouse for a New York City Parks Department golf course. They named the place Enchanted Garden, and before long the two owners were welcoming 2,000 people there every weekend. The success of Enchanted Garden got them thinking they could go even bigger and better with a club in Manhattan.

They found a location at 254 West 54th Street, a former opera house built in 1927. The opera house closed in 1930, a victim of the stock market crash a year earlier. The place changed theatrical hands several times until 1943, when CBS showed up. For the next 33 years, CBS used it as a radio and television studio, producing a number of shows there, including *Ted Mack and the Original Amateur Hour, The Perry Como Show, The Arthur Godfrey Show, The $64,000 Question, Candid Camera, To Tell the Truth, I've Got a Secret, What's My Line?, Beat the Clock, Name that Tune, Captain Kangaroo*, and *Password*.

CBS moved out in 1973, and by 1977 the area had become a place to avoid unless you were looking for recreational drugs or prostitutes. Despite that, Rubell and Schrager immediately recognized the potential of the venue and soon signed a lease. It might not have been the perfect location, but they would make it work perfectly.

To do that, though, the club had to look just right. That task was handed off to architects Scott Bromley and Ron Dowd, along with set-designer Richie Williamson and Tony-award-winning lighting designers Jules Fisher and Paul Marantz. The team did not disappoint. A bolt of lightning couldn't make the cavernous 300 by 200-foot nightclub look like it had more energy. The dazzling lights, brilliant colors, and expansive 5,400-square-foot parquet dance floor got people on their feet and gyrating to the beat of the latest disco hit spun by a DJ who knew how to get everyone high on music. And because the original theater stage and balcony remained

A crowd of people in 1978 hoping to get invited into Studio 54. (Photo by John Barrett/PHOTOlink/Alamy Stock Photo)

part of the $400,000 redesign, those who preferred to watch rather than dance had great spots to view all the action.

The doors opened on April 26, 1977. Rubell and Schrager named the place Studio 54, a reflection of its location on 54th Street. Incredibly, the club didn't yet have a liquor license. Not to be deterred, they solved the problem that night and every night thereafter for about a year by getting a temporary catering permit each day.

From the get-go, Studio 54 attracted superstars like wild honey attracts hungry bears. The list of big-time celebrities who danced the night away there reads like a who's who of anybody who was anyone in the late 1970s. The list included Barbara Streisand, Elton John, Liza Minnelli, Stevie Wonder, Cher, Mick Jagger, Faye Dunaway, Andy Warhol, Olivia Newton-John, Truman Capote,

Ian Schrager (left) and Steve Rubell, circa 1978. (Photo by Adam Scull/Alamy Stock Photo)

John Belushi, Elizabeth Taylor, and Mohammed Ali. They were joined by Jacqueline Kennedy Onassis, John Kennedy, Jr., Michael Jackson, Bette Midler, John Travolta, Diana Ross, Salvador Dali, Oscar de la Renta, Farrah Fawcett, Al Pacino, Calvin Klein, Shirley MacLaine, Joe Namath, Dolly Parton, and Sylvester Stallone – among many others.

On any given night, celebrities could show up at the door and, once recognized, walk right in. Hopefuls waiting on the other side of a velvet rope had to wait for an invite from the doormen. Rubell sometimes joined the doormen to help with the selection process. You wouldn't get in unless you had what was considered the "right look," which typically meant those showing a good measure of energy, enthusiasm, and above-average eye-appeal.

Financially, Studio 54 was a golden goose right from the start. It was mostly a cash business, and the money flowed through the front door like a river at flood stage. Those lucky enough to get in paid a $10 cover charge, the equivalent of about $45 today. And drinks didn't come cheap. An average weeknight would see 1,500 customers inside. A typical weekend night would host 2,000. For Rubell and Schrager, life was very good. But that was about to change.

In early December 1978, Rubell made the mistake of boasting to the press that Studio 54 made $7 million in its first year and that "only the Mafia made more money." Considering that the IRS was aware that the two owners each paid only $8,000 in taxes in 1977, the comment immediately raised red flags at the agency.

Soon the Feds were sniffing around, and it didn't take long for them to realize something smelled fishy. On the morning

The Roundabout Theater now houses the venue formerly occupied by Studio 54. (Photo by author)

of December 14th, IRS agents raided Studio 54 and at the end of an all-day search carted off several filing cabinets filled with an assortment of records. They also found three ounces of cocaine on Ian Schrager, who was promptly charged with possession.

On June 28, 1979, Rubell and Schrager were indicted on federal income tax charges that involved more than $2.5 million skimmed from Studio 54 receipts over three and a half years. A few months later, on November 2, 1979, in Federal District Court in Manhattan, Rubell and Schrager pleaded guilty to charges of evading personal and corporate income taxes. At their sentencing on January 18, 1980, they each received fines of $20,000 along with three-and-a-half-year prison sentences.

To mark the closing of Studio 54, Rubell and Schrager held a gala goodbye bash on February 2, 1980, billing the event as "The

End of Modern-Day Gomorrah." Some 2,000 people showed up, including Andy Warhol, Richard Gere, Reggie Jackson, Bianca Jagger, and Sylvester Stallone. Diana Ross serenaded the soon-to-be-incarcerated pair. Lisa Minelli sang "New York, New York." Everyone there knew it was the end of an era.

Two days later, Rubell and Schrager headed off to a minimum-security prison at Maxwell Air Force Base in Montgomery, Alabama. Later that year, on November 28, 1980, they sold Studio 54 for $4.75 million to Mark Fleischman, a New York City hotel owner and developer. After serving 14 months of their 42-month sentence, the pair was released on April 17, 1981.

The club reopened under Fleischman in September of 1981 to some success, but it never regained the unique spark it had under Rubell and Schrager. In 1986, it closed for good. The place that once steamed and sparkled and sizzled with celebrity energy became as lifeless as a tomb. For a few years thereafter the building was home to an occasional rock concert, but that run lasted only until the late 1980s when it was once more shuttered and vacant.

After prison, Rubell and Schrager went on to have highly successful careers in real estate. Rubell died from AIDS in 1989 at the age of 45. Schrager currently runs The Ian Schrager Company, where, according to the company website, he "owns, develops, manages, and brands hotels, residential, and mixed-use projects."

Visit 254 West 54th Street today and you'll no longer find the place boarded up. That's because, in 1998, the Roundabout Theater Company moved into the building, bringing it full circle back to its roots as a theater. Since then, the nearly 1,000-seat venue has hosted a number of successful stage shows.

Disco may have been buried along with Studio 54, but if you stand in front of the Roundabout Theater today and listen hard for that unmistakable pulsing beat, you might just pick up the faint sound of a time in Manhattan when all the beautiful people came together to make music history.

Marilyn dazzled us here

A subway grate marks the spot where a photo of Marilyn Monroe and her billowing dress became one of America's most iconic images.

Location: Lexington Avenue between East 51st Street and East 52nd Street
Nearest subway stop: 51st Street Station/Lexington Avenue

....

Shortly after midnight on September 15 1954, Gloria Mosolino Jones stepped onto a subway grate outside the front entrance to Wright's Food on Lexington Avenue.

Gloria, wife of *From Here to Eternity* author James Jones, was working that night as a stand-in for Marilyn Monroe. Assembled in front of Gloria was a phalanx of lights and cameras and dolly tracks all being moved around by a busy film crew working to set up a scene for *The Seven Year Itch*, the latest movie by director Billy Wilder.

The scene they were creating had Marilyn and co-star Tom Ewell strolling north on Lexington Avenue. As the two casually walk along a subway grate, a passing train shoots up a blast of air that sends her pleated white cocktail dress billowing skyward, causing Marilyn to coo, "Do you feel the breeze from the subway? Isn't it delicious?"

For the stand-in gig, Gloria wore a dress to match the one Marilyn would wear for the actual scene. On cue, an electric fan

Marilyn on the subway grate. (Ian Dagnall Computing/ Alamy Stock Photo).

under the grate was turned on to send Gloria's dress billowing. Over the next hour and a half, the fan was used several more times as the crew dialed-in lighting and camera angles.

It wasn't until 1:45 a.m. that the shot was ready to be put to film. By the time Marilyn and Tom Ewell appeared at the grate there were dozens of professional photographers ready to record the event along with what was reported to be a crowd of between 500 and 2,000 onlookers, all straining to get a glimpse of Marilyn. The crowd wasn't a coincidence. Not one to miss an opportunity for free publicity, Wilder had earlier alerted the press to the shoot.

Among the crowd was Marilyn's husband, former New York Yankee superstar Joe DiMaggio. Joe had planned to remain in their room at the St Regis Hotel during the shoot, but the gossip columnist Walter Winchell convinced him to walk over to Lexington Avenue to watch the filming.

For over an hour, Marilyn stood on the grate as the electric fan repeatedly boosted her dress – occasionally well above her shapely hips – appearing at times to be making only a casual effort to keep it under control. Two pairs of white underwear – the bonus pair for extra security – were the only garments she had on under the dress. The mostly male crowd, some of them standing on cars, reportedly roared with delight with each new rush of air. It was past 3 a.m. by the time Wilder finally called it a wrap.

Later it was learned that DiMaggio had become increasingly incensed as the shoot progressed. While the crowd cheered every blast of air to come out of that grate, Joltin' Joe had to stoically

Marilyn and co-star Tom Ewell at the famous grate as film cameras rolled. (Entertainment Pictures/Alamy Stock Photo)

The location as it looks today. (Photo by author)

stand by and watch the onlookers gawp at way too much of his gorgeous wife.

Eventually, he left the set and went back to the St Regis Hotel in what was reported to be a sour mood. Later, when Marilyn returned to their room after the shoot, the two were said to have had a heated argument. He felt she'd made the shoot unnecessarily risqué. She said she was just doing her job. Reports soon circulated that she went to bed that night with bruises. The two returned to Los Angeles later that day, and Marilyn filed for a divorce shortly after.

Ironically, Wilder couldn't use any of the footage from that Lexington Avenue shoot. Between the crowd noise and the saucy images of Marilyn that 1950s censors would surely deem offensive, he later had to reshoot the scene on a sound stage in Los Angeles.

The actual movie scene is a tame version of what unfolded that September night in Manhattan.

However, the still photos taken that night ended up being used to publicize the movie. One shot in particular, taken by Marilyn's good friend Sam Shaw, was not only used for some of the movie posters, but also became one of the most iconic photos ever taken of her.

Wright's Food and the other nearby stores on the block are now gone. But the subway line is still there, along with the same grid of grates. Although there is some dispute as to the exact location of the spot where Marilyn stood, an ambitious researcher has studied old photos of the shoot and concluded that it's almost certainly the fifth grate in from 52nd Street. If you're lucky enough to stand there when a subway train comes ripping by, you just might be rewarded with the same delicious breeze that Marilyn enjoyed on that early mid-town Manhattan morning back in 1954.

Tin Pan Alley: the birthplace of American popular music

Many of the buildings on the street were torn down years ago, but a few still stand as reminders of a remarkable musical era.

Location: West 28th Street, between 6th Avenue and Broadway
Nearest subway stop: 28th Street Station/Broadway

....

Before there were phonograph cylinders, or phonograph records, or radios, or televisions, or cassette-tape players, or CDs, or streaming services, there was something called parlor music: a popular form of entertainment that enjoyed its heyday between 1850 and 1920. Throughout most of that period, unless you could attend a live musical performance, parlor music was the main way to enjoy a good song.

As the name suggests, parlor music was played in the parlor at home, typically by a family member. A piano was used most often, but a violin or flute or banjo or any other instrument could do just as well. And if someone didn't have an instrument to play, they'd simply belt out a song with the best singing voice they could muster.

However, before anyone in the parlor could enjoy a song, they'd need a copy of the sheet music to provide the tune and lyrics. And that's how Tin Pan Alley finds its way into this story.

One of the brownstones that made up
Tin Pan Alley on West 28th Street, circa
1900 (Wikimedia Commons)

The moniker Tin Pan Alley has a couple of different meanings. In its original context, it described the concentration of music publishers that were found in Manhattan during the late nineteenth and early twentieth centuries. Nowadays, it's also used as a shorthand for any neighborhood in any town or city where you might find music publishers setting up shop to create music for popular songs (Denmark Street in London, England is one example).

The location of Manhattan's Tin Pan Alley has moved a few times over the years. In the mid-1800s it could be found around 14th Street, whereas by 1930 it had worked its way north, near Times Square. During its golden years, from about 1893 to 1910, Tin Pan Alley was located on West 28th Street between 6th Avenue and Broadway. Granted, a good many music publishers could be found at other locations throughout lower Manhattan back then, but not in numbers that matched the dozens that were nestled together on 28th Street at the time.

Indeed, by 1900, West 28th had the largest concentration of popular music publishers ever found anywhere. The number peaked in 1907, when there were 38 publishers on the street. Thanks to the musical energy that coursed through all those brownstones, Tin Pan Alley at that location is now considered the birthplace of American songwriting.

Exactly how the name Tin Pan Alley came to be is still in dispute. As early as 1882, the term "tin-pan piano" was used to describe any inexpensive and aged upright piano that had seen better days and was now sounding "tinny." From there, it's easy to imagine someone nicknaming a street filled with music publishers playing old upright tin-pan pianos as "tin pan alley." It's also possible to imagine the cacophony of all the upright pianos on 28th Street playing different songs at the same time. The resulting noise may well have sounded like everyone in those brownstones was doing little more than banging on a collection of old tin pans.

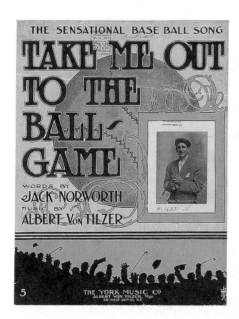

The cover of the sheet music to Take Me Out To The Ball Game, published circa 1908 by The York Music Co. (Wikimedia Commons)

Many of those brownstones were originally built as private homes in the early to mid-1800s. As the years went by, homeowners began to head further north on the island in search of new ground. When they moved out, the homes were subdivided into office space and the music publishers moved in, setting up their shops mostly on the upper floors. The ground floors were home to all sorts of different businesses; restaurants, taverns, grocery stores, and the like. Also showing up in the neighborhood were many flower shops, and years later the area would become known as Manhattan's flower district.

The music publishers commissioned melodies and lyrics for the next parlor music hit from a roster of composers. If the publishers thought a song had potential, they'd print it as sheet music for distribution throughout the United States. Many composers were on staff, but freelancers often showed up on 28th Street with a new tune in hand, scratched out on notepaper. If the song caught the ear of a publisher, the composer would walk away with a contract that would earn them a royalty based on sales.

Of course, those early music publishers had to do more than simply print and distribute sheet music. They needed people to buy it. And before that could happen, the American public had to hear the music in order to decide if they liked it or not.

In the early twentieth century, there were only a few ways to make songs public. Oftentimes, the songwriters themselves would visit theaters, music halls, cabarets, beer gardens, and saloons in an effort to get their music played to an audience. If the song got some toes tapping, the hope was that audience members would dash down to the nearest music store and buy the sheet music.

Publishers often hired musicians to beat those same bushes. Nicknamed "pluggers," they would play the song wherever they could find an audience. If a plugger was really lucky, a vaudeville performer would like the song and play it every night as the show traveled throughout the country. It was marketing in its purest form.

Sheet music was big business back then, and Tin Pan Alley was where most of that business took place. Between 1900 and 1909, over 90 songs enjoyed sales of at least one million copies. Sales peaked in 1910, a year in which some 2 billion copies of sheet music were sold.

That's in large part because the population of affluent Americans had grown significantly after the Civil War ended in 1865. At the same time, the advent of the relatively inexpensive stand-up piano made the instrument more affordable. By 1886, seven out of ten students in American schools were learning to read music; by the end of the century, it's estimated that some 500,000 Americans were learning to play the piano. All this helped to increase the yearly sales of pianos from only few thousand in 1850 to almost 365,000 by 1910. (By way of comparison, about 32,000 pianos were sold each year in the United States between 2015 and 2019, even though our current population is more than three times greater than it was in 1910.)

The first music publisher to show up in the neighborhood was M. Witmark and Sons, arriving at 49 and 51 West 28th Street in 1893 after moving from 14th Street. Others soon followed.

A remarkable number of hit songs came out of Tin Pan Alley in those golden years, thanks mostly to the songwriters who created them and the publishers who printed, sold, and distributed them. Many of those songs became classics that remain popular to this

The cover of the sheet music to When Irish
Eyes Are Smiling, published in 1912 by
M. Witmark and Sons (Wikimedia
Commons)

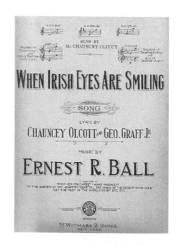

day, including "Take Me Out to the Ball Game" (The York Music,
40 28th Street, 1908), "By the Light of the Silvery Moon" (Jerome
H. Remick, 45 28th Street, 1909), "Sweet Adeline," and "When
Irish Eyes Are Smiling" (both M. Witmark & Sons, 51 28th Street,
1903 and 1912).

It's important to point out that despite all the wonderful and
uplifting songs that came out of Tin Pan Alley, one particular genre
can today only be seen as toxic. It evolved from the minstrel shows
that were popular in the 1890s: shows which typically featured white
entertainers in blackface singing songs that mocked and degraded
African-Americans, usually by presenting them as likeable, happy-
go-lucky characters who were mostly lazy and dimwitted.

By the turn of the century, minstrel songs were in high demand.
White composers and even a few African-American composers
quickly went to work writing more. Over the next two decades,
music publishers sold millions of copies of such songs, which were
often packaged with shamefully racist artwork. Fortunately, by

the 1920s, the genre had begun to fall out of favor and the most offensive titles slipped out of circulation.

Tin Pan Alley continued to experience other changes. The new century brought with it a new and exciting technology – the phonograph – which it would prove to have a considerable impact on sheet music sales. With a phonograph in the parlor, anyone could listen to the latest songs without any need for an instrument. In turn, with no need for an instrument, the demand for sheet music began to drop.

As a result, by about 1910 more and more sheet-music publishers were also getting into the record business. That meant they had to follow the entertainment crowd further north. By 1920, most were gone from West 28th Street.

Only five buildings from Tin Pan Alley remain today – 47, 49, 51, 53, and 55 West 28th Street. (Photo by author)

One intact block of five adjacent buildings on the north side of the street still remains – 47, 49, 51, 53, and 55 West 28th Street. In 2019, all were scheduled to be demolished and most likely replaced with high-rises. But concerned citizens, including the Save Tin Pan Alley initiative and the 29th Street Neighborhood Association, raised a ruckus and the New York City Landmarks Preservation Commission stepped in to save them all from the wrecking ball.

If you walk West 28th Street between 6th Avenue and Broadway today, you almost certainly won't hear a single piano. But let your mind drift back in time, and you might be able to imagine a fresh-faced composer skipping up the front steps of one of those brownstones, new song gripped tightly in hand, ink still not fully dry, hoping to turn the head of a publisher with the next big hit.

The first Oreo cookie was baked here

It happened over a hundred years ago – and anyone with a sweet tooth has been smiling ever since.

Location: Chelsea Market, 75 9th Avenue between 15th Street and 16th Street
Nearest subway stop: 14th Street Station/8th Avenue

....

The Oreo is the world's favorite store-bought cookie. What's not to like? It's chocolaty, it's crunchy, and it's blessed with a delightful layer of sweet, gooey icing squeezed in between the two cookie halves. If you're a normal human being, no matter how hard you try, you can't eat just one.

Mondelez International, Inc., the current owner of the Oreo brand, proudly claims that roughly 34 billion Oreo cookies are sold each year in more than 100 countries. The United States alone accounts for 10 billion of that number, almost one-third of all sales.

The Oreo has roots that go back to 1890 when a number of small bakeries joined together to form the New York Biscuit Company. Soon the company was constructing several multistory bakery buildings on 10th Avenue between 15th and 16th Streets in Manhattan's Chelsea neighborhood. Then, in 1898, the New York Biscuit Company merged with the American Biscuit and

Manufacturing Company to form the National Biscuit Company with headquarters in Chicago. In 1906, the headquarters moved to the Chelsea complex. In 1913, the company built an 11-story bakery on 10th Avenue across the street from the complex (see photo on page 74). By 1921 they had purchased and constructed buildings on the entire block bounded by 9th and 10th Avenues and 15th and 16th Streets. At the time it was the world's biggest bakery.

The cookie we love to love. (Photo by author)

In 1912, the company had been looking to copy the Hydrox, a chocolate sandwich cookie invented in 1908 by the Loose-Wiles Biscuit Company in Kansas City, Missouri. The Hydrox quickly became a hot-seller, and the National Biscuit Company wanted a piece of the market. In short order they created a clone and gave it the name Oreo. (Despite a good deal of speculation over the years, no one seems to know for sure where the name Oreo came from.) The official full name of the cookie has changed several times since then. It was introduced as the Oreo Biscuit. In 1921, it became the Oreo Sandwich. In 1937, it was the Oreo Crème Sandwich. And in 1974, it was called the Oreo Chocolate Sandwich Cookie, the handle it still uses today.

Thanks to National Biscuit's deep pockets and powerful marketing department, it didn't take long for Oreo to eclipse Hydrox in sales. The Hydrox is still around today, although its sales are only a small fraction of Oreo's monster numbers. But that hasn't stopped a long-running debate between aficionados of the two brands, with each camp arguing they own bragging rights to the world's best tasting chocolate sandwich cookie.

The National Biscuit Company began using the name Nabisco on some of its products as early as 1909, but it wasn't until 1971 that the company officially changed its corporate name to Nabisco, at least partly to avoid confusion with the television and radio operations of the National Broadcasting Company (NBC). Over the years, in addition to the Oreo, Nabisco introduced a number of other well-known products, including Fig Newtons, Graham Crackers, Barnum's Animal Crackers, Lorna Doones, Mallomars, Saltines, and Vanilla Wafers.

A National Biscuit Company building, circa 1913. The entrance under the company sign is on 11th Avenue between 15th Street and 16th Street. The other side of the building is bordered by 10th Avenue. This building still stands today. The entire block today from 10th Avenue to 9th Avenue is filled out with several more former National Biscuit Company buildings. (Library of Congress Prints and Photographs Division)

Nabisco's days in Chelsea became numbered in the 1930s with the arrival of a new and revolutionary oven design for baking cookies on a commercial scale. Instead of ovens that moved cookies vertically as they baked, the new ovens used thin, steel conveyor belts to move the cookies horizontally. And because long, horizontal conveyor belts needed long, single-story buildings, all the multistoried buildings owned by the National Biscuit Company in Chelsea were no longer suited for modern ovens. It wasn't long before the company began to build a new state-of-the-art single-story bakery

The Chelsea Market entrance at 9th Avenue and 15th Street. The Market takes up the entire block of old National Biscuit Company buildings located between 9th and 10th Avenues and West 15th and West 16th Streets. (Photo by author)

in the roomy suburbs. The entire bakery complex in Chelsea, consisting of 22 buildings over 2 million square feet, was sold to an investor in 1959.

In 1990, an investment syndicate brought most of the buildings and in 1997 opened the Chelsea Market. The ground floor features food shops, a food court, and a shopping mall. Office space fills the upper floors. The complex stretches throughout the entire footprint of the old Nabisco bakery and has over a million square feet of retail space.

The old bones of the Nabisco bakery are very much in evidence there as the original walls and ceilings are exposed throughout for everyone to appreciate. Each year more than 9 million people visit. In 2018, Google bought the Chelsea Market property for a reported $2.8 billion.

You'll be hard-pressed to find Oreos for sale at Chelsea Market today; the general fare there tends to be a bit more upscale. That's too bad. After all, what could be more appropriate than to munch on a few of those delightful cream-filled treats while walking through the bowels of the old National Biscuit Company – the place that first gave us that classic American cookie more than 100 years ago?

Thomas' English Muffins Got Started here

The nooks and crannies, too.

Location: 163 9th Avenue between West 19th Street and West 20th Street
Nearest subway stop: 23rd Street Station/8th Avenue
Secondary location: 337 West 20th Street between 8th and 9th Avenues
Nearest subway stop: 23rd Street Station/8th Avenue

The history of the English muffin is somewhat convoluted, but it's generally agreed that in Great Britain and Ireland a version of it dates back at least 1,000 years to when small, round, yeast-risen flatbreads were cooked individually in ring molds on a hot, flat stone. It's believed the word "muffin" evolved from the Low German word "muffin," meaning "little cake." In 1703, the word muffin, spelled "moofin," shows up for the first time in print as part of a collection of letters belonging to John Ray, the famous English naturalist. So, in one form or another, the muffin has been around for a long, long time.

Those early flatbread muffins were split in half by hand to be enjoyed either plain or, more typically, with butter or honey. Any leftovers were later split and toasted to reheat. Since the electric toaster wouldn't be invented until 1893, muffins were traditionally toasted on a hot stone in front of a fire, or on a wire frame over the flames, or stuck on sticks to be held over the hot coals.

Today we define the English muffin as a round flatbread cooked on both sides on a griddle – usually using ring molds – and then split by hand or with a fork. To reheat, they're usually toasted in an electric pop-up toaster. Nowadays, in addition to butter or honey, we add all sorts of toppings to them, such as jam, jelly, marmalade, peanut butter, pizza sauce and mozzarella cheese (with perhaps some sausage or pepperoni for good measure), and of course a combination of poached eggs, sliced ham, and hollandaise sauce to create the delectable classic we call Eggs Benedict.

Exactly when the flatbread muffin showed up in America isn't clear, but we know Thomas Jefferson enjoyed them at Monticello.

Samuel Bath Thomas' Manhattan bakery made the English muffin a breakfast staple everywhere it was sold. (Photo by author)

Also uncertain is when the flatbread muffin became commonly known as the English muffin. At some point, bakers of flatbread muffins in America probably added the word "English" to avoid confusing the product with the American muffin – the cake-like treat baked in an oven using cupcake molds that produce an oversized muffin top.

Webster's Dictionary suggests that the first recorded use of the term "English muffin" was in 1858. It was certainly in use by September 22, 1859, when an advertisement in The Buffalo (New York) *Daily Republic* publicized Thomas' (no relation) Dining Saloon with a bill of fare that included "Hot English muffins, morning and evening." Later, a classified ad in the *New York Herald* newspaper dated September 17, 1862, would simply read: "Wanted – An English muffin and crumpet baker. Apply to 910 Broadway."

Across the pond, an English muffin is simply called a muffin. In the eighteenth and nineteenth centuries they were often sold on the street and door-to-door by one-man vendors called muffin men. The muffin men were ubiquitous enough to inspire a nursery rhyme and song that's still popular on both sides of the Atlantic:

Do you know the muffin man?
The muffin man, the muffin man.
Do you know the muffin man?
Who lives in Drury Lane.

For a good part of the 1800s, hungry Americans showed little interest in English muffins. But then, in 1872, a 26-year-old

Thomas made a mountain of English muffins in this building at 163 Ninth Avenue between the years 1880 and 1915. (Photo by author)

immigrant from Plymouth, England, named Samuel Bath Thomas arrived in New York City looking for a job.

Thomas soon found work at a local bakery and, a year later, married Janet "Jenny" Paton, a recent immigrant from Scotland. Within seven years the two had four daughters: Elizabeth ("Bessie"), Kathleen, Roberta, and Mary.

In 1880 Thomas opened his own business, a wholesale bakery at 163 9th Avenue. It must have been a good location because he ended up staying there for the next 35 years. During this time, in addition to the usual assortment of common baked breads, Thomas also began selling a much-enjoyed treat he remembered from earlier days in England – the flatbread muffin – calling them English muffins.

Apparently, it didn't take long for Manhattanites to develop a taste for Thomas' muffins, perhaps because he had a better recipe than other bakers or perhaps because it was simply a welcome change from dry toast. Whatever the reason, his English muffins were soon being stocked in local stores, restaurants, and hotels. Customers loved them and eventually they could be bought as far away as the Bronx, Brooklyn, and Queens.

Janet died at their West 22nd Avenue house in 1908 at the age of 60. In 1911 Thomas went back to England for health reasons, planning to stay for two years. However, he didn't return to New York until October 1919, claiming on his passport application at the American Embassy in London that he had been unable to come back earlier because of "German submarine risks." His concern was not unreasonable. World War I had started while he was in England and, by the time the war ended in 1918, German U-boats had sunk

In 1914, Thomas opened up a second bakery here at 337 West 20th Street and today a plaque attached to the front of the building honors its heritage. The address currently houses private apartments. (Photo by author)

more than 5,500 merchant and fishing vessels, 10 battleships, 18 cruisers, a number of smaller naval ships.

In 1914, while he was still in England, Thomas opened a new bakery at 337 West 20th Street. The building once had a foundry operating in the basement, a feature that would likely be welcomed by anyone looking to open a commercial bakery. It operated there until at least 1920.

Eventually the building was converted to co-op apartments, and in 2006 the owners of the first-floor apartment made a fascinating discovery. While undertaking renovations that included opening a back wall, they discovered a 15 by 20-foot brick oven that extended out and under the rear courtyard. No doubt countless loaves of Samuel Thomas' bread had come out of those ovens. It's not known whether a muffin griddle was ever found.

To honor its place in culinary history, the Chelsea Historic District awarded a plaque that can now be viewed on front of the building. It reads: "The Muffin House. Built as a foundry c. 1850, Samuel Bath Thomas (1855–1919) converted the ovens for his English Muffin Bakery in the early 20th century. The arched brick structures remain below the courtyard garden."

Samuel Thomas continued making bread and English muffins at the West 20th Street location until he died at age 71 on October 28, 1919, just 16 days after returning from England. One newspaper obituary simply described him as a wholesale dealer in health bread.

Despite the death of its founder, the Thomas' bakery business continued to flourish. In 1922 the company was incorporated with $10,000 in capital from his daughter Elizabeth, his nephew Robert

S. Swanson (the son of Janet's sister Elizabeth), and William E. Bachtenkirch.

In or around 1924, under the name SB Thomas, Inc., they built a brand-new bakery in nearby Long Island City (Queens) New York. A second bakery with over 100,000 square feet of space was built in Totowa, New Jersey, in 1961, costing about $1.2 million.

Up until 1970, SB Thomas, Inc. was still privately owned and Robert S. Swanson's son, Robert, Jr., was serving as president of the company. That same year the company was bought by CPC International, Inc. for $20 million in stock. At the time, the English muffin was known mostly in the Northeast, and CPC soon began an aggressive advertising campaign to introduce the English muffin to the rest of the United States. By 1983, they had five plants with 1,800 employees and annual sales of $125 million. A total of 25 products shipped daily to 30,000 stores throughout the U.S.

In 2001, Thomas' was acquired by the Canadian company George Weston Ltd. At the time, Thomas' had annual sales of approximately $300 million.

Bimbo, the Mexican multinational corporation headquartered in Mexico City, bought Weston Foods in 2009. Americans were still chowing down on English muffins, especially Thomas'. Indeed, in 2019, over 115 million Americans consumed Thomas' English muffins, generating roughly $500 million in sales. By comparison, about 16 million Americans opted instead for Pepperidge Farm English muffins, Thomas' nearest competitor.

Some 140 years after Samuel Thomas opened his wholesale bakery on 9th Avenue in Chelsea, we still have a big thing for those little old-time flatbreads. Next time you pop one in the toaster, you might want to take a moment to thank Samuel for firing up his griddle those many years ago and introducing us to such a delightfully tasty treat.

The Triangle Shirtwaist Company fire

146 workers died here, most of them young women.

Location: 23–29 Washington Place, between Greene Street and Washington Square East
Nearest subway stop: West 4th Street/Washington Square Station

At about 4:30 p.m. on Saturday, March 25, 1911, some 450 employees of The Triangle Shirtwaist Company were minutes away from the end of their shift and heading home. They had just received their weekly pay, and everyone was looking forward to Sunday and a well-earned day of rest.

As the name suggests, The Triangle Shirtwaist Company made waists (also called shirtwaists): woman's long-sleeve, button-down blouses. Shirtwaists were in high style at the time and the place was very busy.

The company occupied the eighth, ninth, and tenth floors óf the ten-story Asch Building in Greenwich Village. Most of workers were women, many of them Italian and Jewish immigrants in their late teens and early twenties. Some were as young as 14. Few spoke English.

Each floor of the building measured about 90 by 100 feet. The company executives, including the two owners, were in offices on the tenth floor along with another 75 employees who were responsible for pressing, packing, and shipping the shirts. The floor below, the ninth floor, had about 225 workers, most of them women who sat elbow-to-elbow at long wooden tables feeding fabric into belt-driven sewing machines at breakneck speed. Roughly 150 employees, mostly women, were on the eighth floor, working at cutting tables and more sewing machines.

The 10-year-old building had walls, floors, and staircases designed to be fireproof. The contents, though – not so much. Highly flammable cotton fabric was everywhere, especially on the eighth and ninth floors where the shirts were cut and sewn. Work in progress was stacked in piles. Long wooden troughs under the cutting tables were filled with scraps. Bins and baskets held extra bits and pieces of material. Even more odds and ends were scattered about the tables and floor. Then, too, there were paper patterns all about, hanging above the cutting tables.

It took less than 40 minutes for firemen to extinguish the blaze after it started. But those minutes were remarkably deadly. (Photo courtesy of the Kheel Center, Cornell University)

Each floor had two exit doors located in diagonally opposite corners of the building. The doors led to narrow stairwells: one going down to Green Street, the other down to Washington Place.

There were also two passenger elevators and two freight elevators. An outside fire escape was located in a light court on the northeast side of the building, accessible through a window on each of the three floors.

On the day of the fire, on the eighth and ninth floors, the door to the Washington Place stairwell was locked, a routine practice for the company. Managers worried about employee pilferage, so everyone on those floors always had to exit the building using the Greene Street stairwell after having their handbags checked.

The fire started on the eighth floor at about 4:30 p.m., coming to unholy life in a pile of scraps on the floor near the Green Street stairwell. The exact cause was never determined with certainty; perhaps it was a carelessly discarded cigarette (although smoking was forbidden, on occasion one of the men would be seen sneaking one), perhaps it was a spark from a machine, perhaps something else.

Employees tried to douse the fire with water buckets kept on the floor for just such an event, but the effort was futile. Paper patterns hanging nearby immediately caught fire. In just moments the blaze became unstoppable.

The Green Street door was wide open at the time, creating a draft that pushed the flames toward the airshaft near the wall on the opposite side of the building. Seeing the fire growing before them, all the workers on the eighth floor managed to get out using either the Greene Street stairwell, the elevators, or the fire escape.

For some, the only way to escape the flames was to jump. No one survived the fall. (Photo courtesy of the Kheel Center, Cornell University)

Before fleeing, someone on the eighth floor had the presence of mind to phone the tenth floor and warn management of the growing conflagration. Thanks to the call, all of the tenth-floor employees, including owners Isaac Harris and Max Blanck, were able to take the Green Street stairs to the roof and escape to an adjoining building. An effort to call the ninth floor, however, never got through.

For the 225 or so workers still on the ninth floor, the first sign of trouble was the wisps of smoke coming up the stairwells at about 4:40 p.m. Then, almost immediately, flames roared up from below through the airshaft near the north corner. In seconds that entire corner of the floor was on fire.

Some ninth-floor workers dashed to safety by taking the Greene Street stairwell to the roof. Others got out using the passenger and freight elevators, which were able to make a few runs before the fire halted any more attempts at getting to the top floors. By 4:45 p.m., all the elevators and the Greene Street stairwell were impassible from heavy smoke and flames.

Fed by hundreds of pounds of fabric, the ninth floor quickly became an inferno. Some workers made it to the fire escape, but before anyone could get down to street level, it completely collapsed under the added weight. Two dozen people died from the fall.

With the doorway to the Greene Street stairwell now blocked by flames, the elevators out of operation, and the fire escape a crumpled heap, the only remaining exit was the locked Washington Place stairwell. Reportedly, a male supervisor with a key was able to fight his way through the crowd of panicked workers and unlock the door, but it opened inward, and by that time the crush of workers against the door made it impossible to open.

Now, with no safe means of escape, and the fire raging everywhere about them, some workers attempted to slide down the cables of one of the two passenger elevators. A few workers were successful, but most lost their grip and fell. Others may simply have chosen to jump down the shaft rather than face the approaching flames. Or, perhaps, in the crush of panicked humanity, some were accidentally pushed into the opening. One way or another, 19 workers died in this elevator shaft, piling up on the roof of the elevator car on the first floor.

The alarm reached the fire department at 4:45 p.m. At 4:47 p.m., when the first officer in command arrived in a horse-drawn fire wagon, he could see the entire eighth floor engulfed in flames. He also saw something very startling. On the ninth floor, workers desperately trying to escape the smoke and flames were standing on the narrow ledges outside some of the windows. He immediately sent in a second alarm that was recorded at 4:48 p.m. A third alarm followed seven minutes later, then a fourth one at 5:10 p.m.

Several firemen carrying hoses quickly entered the Greene Street and Washington Place stairwells and started up. The trucks raised their ladders, but the highest they could reach was the sixth floor, 30 feet short of the ninth floor.

Watching from above, terrified workers on the ledges now knew any hope of rescue was gone. Driven out by the choking smoke and scorching heat, many chose their one remaining option. They jumped.

Some women managed to hold out until their dresses caught fire. As they fell, onlookers described them as looking like human torches. Before long, as more bodies crashed to the ground, water from the firehoses washing along the sidewalk began to run red with blood. Efforts by firefighters to use safety nets proved futile as the eighty-foot drop created much too much impact force. Some 40 workers ended up falling or jumping from the ninth floor. None survived.

Once inside the building, firefighters were able to control the fire fairly quickly. It was all over by 5:10 p.m., no more than 30 to 40 minutes after it started. But for workers on the ninth floor, those minutes were deadly. Firemen found the charred remains of about 60 bodies there. No one was found alive.

A total of 146 victims went to the morgue that night: 123 women and 23 men. Family members then faced the gruesome

The burnt-out remains of work tables and sewing machines on the ninth floor. (Photo courtesy of the Kheel Center, Cornell University)

task of trying to identify their loved ones, oftentimes relying on little more than a wrist watch, a piece of bridgework, a small item of jewelry, or a recognizable shoe to confirm a victim's name.

On Thursday, April 6th, despite a steady rain, the victims were remembered by more than 250,000 people who turned out to support an estimated 120,000 marchers, many of them women working in nearby lofts and factories. The march moved through Washington Square Park and up 5th Avenue before eventually working its way to Madison Square Park where it ended. Stunned by the tragedy, New Yorkers opened their hearts and wallets like never before to create a fund for the victims' families.

The fire led to a massive public outcry for safer workplaces. Within weeks, the Factory Investigating Commission was established. That

The Asch Building is now called the Brown Building. It's owned by New York University. (Photo by author)

led to much improved fire-safety laws. Buildings would now have sprinkler systems and be subject to frequent inspections, exit doors had to be unlocked during working hours and open outward, and regular fire drills were required.

The Asch Building still stands, although it is known today as the Brown Building. It's owned by New York University and currently houses the Biology and Chemistry departments. Remarkably, the exterior today looks much the same as it did on the morning of the fire. Every year, on March 25th, the fire victims are remembered at a solemn ceremony held on the sidewalk outside the Brown Building. A single bell tolls as each name is read – a tribute to those whose deaths spurred greater workplace safety for future generations.

The *General Slocum* Steamboat Fire

957 people died – most of them German-American women and children on a church outing – after their ship caught fire in the East River shortly after departing Manhattan.

Departure location: East River Park
Nearest subway stop: Delancey Street/Essex Street Station (from the
station, the walk to the departure location is about 0.9 miles)

Everyone waiting in line had been looking forward to the excursion for months. The Manhattan winter that year had been, as usual, long and cold, followed by a typically damp and muddy spring. By June 15, 1904, with the warming rays of a morning sun filtering across the East River, some 1,358 people were itching to get the day going. Almost all of them were from St. Mark's Evangelical Lutheran Church at 325 East 6th Street.

St. Mark's was located in the heart of what was then called Little Germany, a neighborhood in the Lower East Side of Manhattan that in 1904 stretched from Broadway to the East River and from 14th Street to Grand Street. In 1900, some 750,000 Germans lived in New York City, many of them in Little Germany. At the time, only two cities in the world – Vienna, Austria; and Berlin, Germany

– could claim a larger German-speaking population. Avenue B in Manhattan was known as German Broadway. Social clubs, singing societies, beer halls, shooting clubs, grocery stores, restaurants, and theaters nearby all catered to German proclivities.

In the 1800s, many of the Irish, Italian, and Jewish immigrants arriving in New York came with little education and few, if any, special skills. German arrivals tended to be better educated and often brought with them a trade. They worked throughout New York City as tailors, bakers, carpenters, furniture makers, shoemakers, beer brewers, and machinists, jobs that earned them decent wages in their adopted country right from the get-go. Indeed, most of the parishioners from St. Mark's enjoyed a standard of living that was considered relatively comfortable.

The steamboat General Slocum. (Shutterstock)

The East Third Street Recreation Pier on the East River (circa 1910) where the General Slocum boarded passengers on that fateful day. It's believed the terrible fire started just a short time after the steamer departed from the pier. (Collection of the New-York Historical Society)

That morning, a good part of St. Mark's congregation patiently stood in line on the East Third Street Recreational Pier, watching in awe and anticipation as the 230-foot steamer *General Slocum* – her two 31-foot-diameter paddles churning the dark water into a rolling boil – slowly pushed up the East River and settled in alongside the pier. Each June for 17 years running, to celebrate the end of the church-school year, St. Mark's held an annual picnic outing: a boat trip up the East River to Locust Grove at Eaton's Neck on Long Island Sound, a two-hour excursion each way.

Because it was a Wednesday, a workday for the husbands and fathers, most of those from St. Mark's waiting to board the ship were women and children. After a day of picnicking, swimming, and games, everyone would be back at the Manhattan pier by nightfall; tired, sunburnt, and contented from their short time in a world far away from the busy streets of Little Germany.

A couple of hours earlier, 66-year-old William Henry Van Schaick had risen from his bunk on the *General Slocum* and begun preparing for a busy day. Van Schaick was captain of the *Slocum*, the only captain she'd ever had, and his reputation stood as one of the best pilots in and about New York Harbor. His bedroom was in the forward section of the ship, which was tied up in Manhattan at the 15th Street dock on the North River (now called the Hudson River). Also sleeping on board that night was the second pilot, the mate, both engineers, a fireman, and some of the crew.

The *Slocum* was a double paddle wheeler – a paddle on each side of the ship – with a wooden hull made of white oak, locust, and yellow pine. It had three wooden passenger decks: the lower one called the main, above it the promenade, and the hurricane on top.

The ship had been plying the waters around Manhattan since it first arrived from a boatyard in Brooklyn 13 years earlier. She was named after Henry Warner Slocum, Sr., a Union general during the Civil War. At the Battle of Gettysburg, his defense of Culp's Hill proved crucial to the Union victory. He was much admired and later elected to the United States House of Representatives from New York.

Owned by the Knickerbocker Steamboat Company, the *General Slocum* was licensed to carry 2,500 passengers. Touted in its earlier days as the "largest and most splendid excursion steamer in New York," the ship had lost some of its luster as it aged and as newer and faster steamers were launched. But it was still considered an impressive and notable ship in and around the harbor.

After the crew washed down the decks that morning, the *Slocum* left the 15th Street dock at about 7 a.m. Aboard were 30 staff members, consisting of crew and caterers. The ship rounded the Battery and arrived at the East Third Street recreation pier on the East River about 8 a.m. Passengers soon began boarding, many of them carrying picnic baskets filled with enough food to fortify the family for the entire day.

As was fashionable at the time, the women wore long dresses, leather shoes, and stylish hats. Children were dressed in their Sunday best, some of them holding small flags to wave along the journey. No more than 10 per cent of the passengers were men older than 21 years of age. Most of the group were children.

It was around 9:30 a.m. when the crew cast off the lines and the great steamer left the recreation pier with first pilot Edward Van Wart at the wheel in the pilot house. Captain Van Schaick was there too, along with second pilot Edward Weaver. Within minutes the steamer was cutting through the water heading north at about 14 knots, a flood tide helping to push them along. On the promenade deck, a German band hired for the occasion played songs from the old country, and some of the passengers began to sing and dance. It had all the makings of a glorious day.

A later investigation determined that the fire began in a 30 by 28-foot storage room that was the third compartment back from the bow and under the main deck. Here, among other miscellaneous items, the fifteen or twenty ship's lights and barrels of lamp oil

The General Slocum at a small pier (unknown location). (Photo courtesy of the National Archives and Records Administration)

were kept. Making it extra volatile, no doubt, were 13 years' worth of spilled oil that had gradually soaked into the wood floor. The night before, members of St. Mark's delivered to the ship two or three barrels of drinking glasses packed in hay to be used during the excursion. After the crew removed the glasses, it was reported that some of the hay had been left scattered all about the room.

Exactly how the fire ignited was never determined with certainty. Some have suggested it was spontaneous combustion of oily rags. Others think it might have been a carelessly discarded match, or perhaps a smoldering cigarette.

The exact time the fire ignited also isn't clear, a detail that would later become an important part of investigations to determine if Captain Van Schaick used his best judgment when choosing when and where to beach his burning ship. The earliest credible report of a problem came from a crewmember who said he first saw signs of fire when the ship reached the north end of Blackwell's Island (now called Roosevelt Island). That would make the time about 10 a.m., 30 minutes after it left the recreation pier, putting the ship just offshore of East 86th Street. Some passengers said they smelled smoke before that, but thought it was coming from the kitchen stoves where clam chowder was cooking for a picnic lunch scheduled to be served after they reached Long Island.

Other passengers and crew had differing opinions on where the ship was when they first learned it was afire. Some said it was near the area of the river called Hell Gate (about 92nd Street). Others said it was further north, near Little Hell Gate (115th Street). Captain Van Schaick and the two pilots insisted the ship was even a bit further north, just off Sunken Meadow Island, although a later investigation would discredit that claim. In any event, at no point on its trip up the East River was the *Slocum* ever much more than a few hundred yards from a shoreline to either its east or west.

You won't find Little Hell Gate and Sunken Meadow Island on any current maps. What is now a single island – called Randalls and Wards Island – was at the time two separate islands; Randalls Island and, just south of it, Wards Island. Between them was a narrow body of water called Little Hell Gate. Just to the east of Randalls was another, smaller, island called Sunken Meadow Island. A landfill project in 1960 filled in Little Hell Gate and also the shoreline up to Sunken Meadow. So, what in the year 1904 was three islands became just one – the Randalls and Wards Island we have today.

Once the fire broke out of the storage room, it quickly moved up a stairway to the main deck. Crew members stunned at the sight tried to turn a fire hose on the blaze, but to their astonishment and dismay, the hose was rotted from years of outside exposure and burst at every kink point. Hardly a drop of water exited the nozzle. An effort to use a rubber hose promptly ended when the crew couldn't attach the coupling to the ship's standpipe. Any hope to control the fire ended right then.

The sight of the smoke and flames immediately set the passengers into a panic. With the forward speed of the ship creating a powerful draft, the flames began to spread from the front of the ship to the back, forcing the passengers on all three decks to move toward the stern.

Many passengers' first instinct was to grab a life jacket. But, to their horror, they immediately realized that the flotation devices

The General Slocum shortly after the fire, sinking in the East River near North Brother Island. (Wikimedia Commons)

were useless. Like the hose, the fabric on the life jackets was rotted from years of outdoor exposure, making them fragile to the point that they tore open when passengers tried to put them on. Worse yet, the life jackets were made from granulated cork. As a result, once the fabric was torn, the old cork inside poured out like sand in an hour glass. Passengers reported seeing people jump into the water wearing a life jacket, only to watch as the hapless souls immediately sank. Rescuers would later note that the surface of the water around the ship was covered with floating particles of cork dust.

Efforts to lower the six lifeboats and two life rafts also proved useless. Some were wired in place and couldn't be easily removed. Others were stuck fast to the ship by a coat of paint that acted like glue. Then, too, the *Slocum* hadn't had a fire drill in a year. And, since most of the crew that day had been recently hired, nearly all of them had never once seen a drill. Not a single lifeboat or life raft was lowered into the water that morning.

There was even more trouble for the passengers. Back then, few people knew how to swim. And the long dresses and layers of wool clothes everyone wore tended to weigh them down once waterlogged. As a result, almost anyone who jumped into the water ended up drowning.

As soon as Captain Van Schaick saw the fire, he decided his best option was to beach the ship on North Brother Island, a point about two miles from Hell Gate and about a quarter mile off East 141st Street in the Bronx. That decision would prove to be very controversial.

Van Schaick felt that beaching at North Brother Island would allow the passengers to jump into the relative safety of shallow water just a few feet from shore. Critics of his decision believe he should have tried to beach the ship sooner, either in Manhattan or the Bronx, because the fire was spreading so quickly.

Later that day, Captain Van Schaick described to the city coroner the last minutes of his struggling vessel:

"I saw a big spurt of flame shoot up and I had enough experience with river fires to know that the General Slocum was doomed. The boat was running perhaps 12 miles per hour. Consequently, the stiff breeze caught the flame and fanned it backward all through the open decks . . . I looked around trying to make up my mind where would be the best place to make a landing. We were just off the sunken meadows. I thought at first of trying to run in there or somewhere along the Bronx shore of the river. But the tide was running so strong that I knew it would be a hard job to swing the boat around at right angles. I was afraid, too, that the steering gear would break down under such a strain and leave us helpless in the middle of the river. A tugboat captain saw me turn the boat a little toward 184th Street on the Bronx side. He yelled at me to keep off, as the fire would ignite the lumber stored there, and the oil tanks on the pier. Then I made up my mind to run for North Brother Island. It seemed the best under the circumstances . . . I may have been wrong, but there was a chance there to beach the Slocum sidewise and give everybody a chance to get off. At the meadows along the Bronx shore that too would have been impossible. There are too many rocks there.

"Then the panic began. I kept my eyes ahead but it was impossible to keep from seeing the frightened scramble for the boat's side, the side towards the Bronx shore. Men fought each other, yelling like mad. Women clawed each other's faces and screamed for their babies. Children cried and screamed and were trampled under foot . . . The rush to the rail on the port side of the boat caused it to heel over a little. This forced a mass of crazed men, women, and children against the guard rail of the upper deck. It broke, and scores – God knows how many – were pitched into the river by the weight from behind . . . I got the General Slocum beached sidewise. It struck 25 feet from shore. Before that the flames had crept to the pilot's house blistering my feet. Van Wart, Weaver, and I got out some way, I can't tell you how, and jumped into the river. We swam to shore, burnt and sick, and stood around until we got a chance to get to the mainland in a small boat."

Dead bodies of passengers arranged in rows on North Brother Island. (Photo by C.C. Langill.)

Captain Van Schaick, along with First Pilot Edward Van Wart, and Second Pilot Edward Weaver were arrested by police a short time after they reached Manhattan.

A reporter on shore who watched the disaster unfold described it as "a spectacle of horror beyond words to express – a great vessel all in flames, sweeping forward in the sunlight, within sight of the crowded city, while her helpless, screaming hundreds were roasted alive or swallowed up in the waves – women and children with their hair and clothing on fire; crazed mothers casting their babies overboard or leaping with them to certain death; wailing children and old men trampled under-foot or crowded over into the water – and the burning steamboat, her whistle roaring for assistance, speeding on for the shore of North Brother Island with a trail of ghastly faces and clutching hands in the tide behind her – gray-haired mothers and tender infants going down to death together."

Unfortunately, Van Schaick wasn't able to beach the ship fully sidewise to the shore as he had planned. Instead, the *Slocum* struck at an angle. It didn't help that he had a ship almost entirely on fire, at the mercy of wind and tricky currents, and panicked passengers dying all around him, while his feet were being scorched by flames licking relentlessly at the pilot house.

The bow ended up in 7 feet of water about 10 to 20 feet from the shore. However, the stern, where most of the passengers were now packed together on the three decks, was sitting in a strong tidal current some 40 to 60 feet from shore and in water that was 10 to 30 feet deep.

With the bow in relatively shallow water and close to shore, the few people there were able to jump to safety. But as the fire continued to overwhelmed the entire ship, those in the stern had no option but to jump into deep water far from shore wearing useless life jackets and unable to swim a single stroke.

To make what was already a horrific event even worse, shortly after the *Slocum* was beached, a portion of the hurricane deck collapsed, sending everyone on that deck either into the fire on the deck below or into water over their heads. It was later estimated that some 400 to 600 people died after the ship was beached, most from drowning.

Within ten minutes of beaching, the entire length of the ship was on fire. Scores of vessels, including tugboats, sloops, fishing boats, and small rowboats, came to help. Dodging the floating bodies of the dead, they pulled floundering passengers out of the water as fast as they could reach them. One tug came so close to the *Slocum* that it, too, briefly caught on fire.

North Brother Island at the time was mostly deserted except for Riverside Hospital, an isolation facility for treating patients with highly infectious diseases like measles, scarlet fever, smallpox, and typhus. When someone at the hospital spotted the burning *Slocum* bearing down on the island, the fire alarm was sounded and dozens of doctors, nurses and other staff members rushed to the shore to offer aid. Even some patients came to help. The hospital response accounted for many of the lives saved.

The New York Police Department later reported that the *General Slocum* had 1,388 people on board that morning – 1,358 passengers (613 adults and 745 children) and 30 crew members or caterers. Of the 1,388 on board, 895 died (893 passengers and 2 crew members) and 62 passengers were declared missing. The number of dead and missing totaled 957. Only 431 survived. Official investigations that followed the fire put several people under the microscope. Indicted for misconduct, negligence, and inattention to duty were Captain Van Schaick along with Frank Barnaby, president of the Knickerbocker Steamboat Company, and three other Knickerbocker executives. Also, two assistant inspectors of the government steamboat-inspection service, Henry Lundberg and John W. Fleming, were indicted for fraud, misconduct, and inattention to duty. Just a few weeks earlier, Lundberg and Fleming had inspected the *Slocum* – including its fire hoses, life jackets, and lifeboats – and declared all of it safe.

On January 27, 1906, a jury found Captain Van Schaick guilty of criminal negligence for failing to run fire drills as required by law.

Charges against the Knickerbocker Steamboat Company and the inspectors were dropped.

Van Schaick was given the maximum prison sentence – 10 years. After serving four of them, President William Howard Taft pardoned him in 1911. He spent his final years at a farm in Troy, N.Y., dying there in 1927 at the age of 90. To the end he remained convinced that under the circumstances he had made the right decision by beaching the *Slocum* at North Brother Island.

The *General Slocum* fire and the terrible loss of life that resulted led to several new safety laws. Passenger vessels would be required to have fireproof bulkheads and hatches, better fire hoses and procedures for regularly testing them, better life jackets and testing procedures, at least one life jacket for each passenger and crew member, lifeboats that could be easily accessed and put into the water, and additional authority for inspectors.

Of the known dead, 61 were so badly burned they were never identified. They were interred in the Lutheran All Faiths Cemetery in Queens, N.Y. On June 15, 1905, exactly one year to the day after the fire, 15,000 people watched as a monument to the 61 unidentified dead was unveiled at the cemetery. Made from marble, the 20-foot monument shows four symbolic figures of despair, grief, courage, and belief in the hereafter. Pulling the cord to unveil the monument was 18-month-old Adella Liebenow. She was six months old on the day of the fire and the youngest survivor of the disaster.

On September 18, 1906, in Tompkins Square Park in what was then the heart of Little Germany, roughly 500 people attended the unveiling of another monument to honor those who died on the *General Slocum*. The gathering included about 150 survivors of

The monument in Tompkins Square Park dedicated to those who died on the General Slocum. (Photo by author)

the disaster. Called the Slocum Memorial Fountain, the nine-foot structure shows two children looking across the water at a steamer passing in the distance. A water fountain with a lionhead spout completes the sculpture. An inscription reads "They were earth's purest children, young and fair." The monument is still there.

In 1940, St. Mark's was sold to the Community Synagogue Max D. Raiskin Center. The synagogue, still at 325 East 6th Street, remains active today. A plaque mounted to the wrought-iron fence honors the victims of the *Slocum* fire.

The East Third Street Recreation Pier is long gone, and the entire stretch of water near there is now part of the John V. Lindsay East River Park. If you go to the park and walk between the two baseball fields that roughly align with the end of Houston Street, you'll be standing where the recreation pier once stretched out into the river to greet the *General Slocum* on June 15, 1904.

Ghostbusters headquarters

It's also home to NYFD's Hook and Ladder Company 8.

Location: 14 North Moore Street and Varick Street
Nearest subway stop: Franklin Street Station/West Broadway

....

Few films have managed to blend action, comedy, and horror quite as well as *Ghostbusters* did when it opened in theaters in 1984. The movie cost about $30 million to make and at last count has brought in almost $300 million worldwide – profit numbers that border on the supernatural.

Starring were Bill Murray, Dan Aykroyd, and Harold Ramis as three paranormal investigators who start a ghost-removal business in Manhattan. The name of their little start-up enterprise is, of course, "Ghostbusters." And they soon find the perfect place to hang their shingle: an empty four-story building that was once a New York City firehouse.

NYFD's Hook and Ladder Company No. 8 in Manhattan's Tribeca neighborhood was reportedly chosen as a shooting location by Dan Aykroyd himself. But because it's a working firehouse the filmmakers could only use the building for exterior shots. Any scenes that take place inside the building were shot on a soundstage in Los Angeles.

The firehouse that's home to NYFD's Hook and Ladder Company 8. (Photo by author)

The firehouse building has a long history. It was designed by Alexander H. Stevens, the city superintendent of buildings, who worked out of the fourth floor of the New York City Fire Headquarters at 157 East 67th Street. When it was built in 1903, the firehouse had two side-by-side doors and was about twice the size of the current structure. Then, in 1913, Varick Street was widened and, to make room for the expanded street, one half of the firehouse was removed. As a result, the building was reduced to the single-doored firehouse we have today.

Hook and Ladder 8 is located less than a mile from where the two World Trade Towers stood. When the call came in on the morning of September 11, 2001, the crew was out of the firehouse and on the scene within minutes. Among them was 43-year-old Lieutenant Vincent G. Halloran, a 20-year veteran of the department and the father of five children with another on the way. He never returned to the station. Lieutenant Halloran was one of 2,753 people who died at the Towers that day, including 343 New York City firefighters.

Where "Crazy Joe" Gallo got whacked

Just before sunup on April 7, 1972, four gunmen walked into Umberto's Clam House restaurant and killed the mob boss.

Location: 129 Mulberry Street
Nearest subway stop: Canal Street Station/Lafayette Street

....

It had been a grand night on the town for mobster Joe Gallo. He'd spent most of it at the Copacabana nightclub on East 60th Street celebrating his 43rd birthday with his new wife Sina Essary, her 10-year-old daughter Lisa, his sister Carmella Fiorello, his bodyguard, Peter Diapoulas, and Peter's friend, Edith Russo.

At the Copa's midnight show, the group sat with actor Jerry Orbach and his wife Marta and comedian David Steinberg. Marta, a writer, was in talks with Gallo about penning his biography. Gallo had gotten to know Jerry Orbach when the actor played a character loosely based on himself in the 1971 film *The Gang That Couldn't Shoot Straight*, a comedy from the book of the same name by journalist and author Jimmy Breslin. The headliner at the Copa that night was Don Rickles and the insult-comedian called out Gallo several times during the show. Joe loved it.

The gathering was a remarkable change from just a year earlier,

114

when Gallo was sitting alone in a New York state prison cell, wrapping up a 10-year sentence for attempted extortion. However, on that night in 1972, as he sat in Manhattan's most popular nightclub, the 5-ft. 6-in. mobster nicknamed "Crazy Joe" must have felt like the toast of the town.

After spending most of the night at the Copa, everyone except the Orbachs and Steinberg headed out to grab a late-night/early-morning bite to eat. It was now about 4:30 a.m. and Gallo wanted to go to Su Ling's restaurant in Chinatown, but by that late hour it was closed. So, they headed for another of his favorite eateries, Luna's at 110 Mulberry Street in Little Italy, but it was also closed. Driving north, they spotted a place at 129 Mulberry that still

The roped-off crime scene in front of Umbertos Clam House just a few hours after Joey Gallo took three bullets while in the restaurant. The bleeding Gallo stumbled out the front door where he then fell and died on the sidewalk. (Jerry Mosey/AP/Shutterstock)

had lights on – Umbertos Clam House – a new restaurant in the neighborhood. Joe had never been there before, and it didn't yet have a liquor license, but it was open and everyone was hungry. So, in they all went.

As fate would have it, standing outside the door when they entered was Joseph Luparelli, a member of the rival Joseph Colombo gang. For about a year, the gang had a contract out on Gallo because they believed he'd ordered the hit on Colombo in 1971 that left the boss almost completely paralyzed.

As the group entered the restaurant, Gallo apparently didn't see Luparelli. Or, perhaps he saw him but didn't know who he was. Either way, the Colombo man saw Gallo and recognized him immediately.

Umbertos Clam House has since moved to 132 Mulberry Street. Today, the 129 Mulberry street location, where the shooting occurred, is home to a restaurant called Da Gennaro. (Photo by author)

Luparelli quickly hoofed it up the street to a Colombo hangout a couple of blocks away. A short time later he came back to Umberto's with a car and four men, all of them packing heat.

As Luparelli waited behind the wheel of the car, the four shooters walked into the restaurant through a back door and immediately opened fire. Gallo and Diapoulas shot back. Police later determined some 20 bullets flew back and forth. Gallo caught three of them. He staggered after the fleeing shooters, but collapsed on the street outside the front door. He died at a nearby hospital a short time later.

Diapoulas was wounded but survived. No one else was hit. The gunmen jumped in the getaway car and disappeared down Mulberry Street. It was all over in a couple of minutes.

Umbertos Clam House is still in business, but it's no longer at 129 Mulberry. They've moved a couple of times since 1972 and today you'll find them at 132 Mulberry. The restaurant Da Gennaro now occupies the infamous 129 Mulberry location where Joe Gallo met his fate.

Gallo's demise wasn't lost on folk singer Bob Dylan. He and Jacques Levy wrote the ballad "Joey" as a tribute to the man who chose to live – and die – by the sword.

The "Bloody Angle" on Chinatown's Doyers Street

A sharp bend in this street earned its macabre name when gangs waged deadly war here.

Location: Between 9 and 13 Doyers Street
Nearest subway stop: Canal Street Station/Centre Street

···

In 1927, when Herbert Asbury wrote *The Gangs of New York*, a book-length exposé that became the inspiration for a 2002 film of the same name directed by Martin Scorsese and starring Daniel Day-Lewis, Leonardo DiCaprio, and Cameron Diaz, the author had this to say about Manhattan's Doyers Street: "The police believe, and can prove it so far as such proof is possible, that more men have been murdered at the bloody angle than at any other place like it in the world."

A claim like that might be hard to confirm. However, no one disputes that a good many young Chinese men died as a result of gang battles that took place throughout Chinatown in Asbury's day, most of them fought to determine control of the gambling, prostitution, protection, and opium trades. The majority of the battles were fought in the relatively small triangular area bounded by Mott Street, Pell Street, and Bowery. Bisecting that triangle is Doyers, a runt of a street not much bigger than an alley that starts at Bowery and ends little more than 100 yards later at Pell.

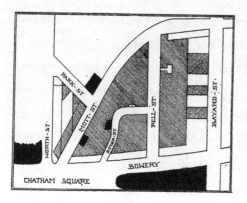

A map of Chinatown (circa 1898). Doyers Street, with its elbow of a bend known as the "Bloody Angle," runs between Bowery and Pell Street. Illustration from the book New York's Chinatown: An Historical Presentation Of Its People And Places by Louis J. Beck, Bohemia Publishing Company, 1898)

About two-thirds of the way from the Bowery, Doyers Street changes direction, going from roughly northwest to due north. The result is a 45-degree bend in the street that became known as the "Bloody Angle," mainly because its centralized geography in Chinatown often put Doyers in or near the eye of the storm whenever the gangs went at it.

Gangs in Chinatown were unique in that each one was associated with its own secret society or fraternal organization known as a "tong." The tongs were ostensibly created for civic good. Mainly, though, they served as headquarters for the gangs, and any civic good generated by them took a big back seat to illegal gang operations.

Of course, a share of the illegal money earned by the gangs went straight into the pockets of crooked cops and politicians who looked the other way as they passed by the gambling houses and opium dens. In general, the gangs could operate with only occasional concern from the law.

The history of Manhattan's Chinatown can be traced to northern California. During the 1850s, some 40,000 Chinese, most of them poor farmers struggling to get by in China during the Taiping Civil War, immigrated to California with dreams of striking it rich in the gold fields. For the vast majority, those dreams ended in disappointment. Pockets empty, some of the immigrants returned home to China, but others remained to toil in silver mines or find other jobs as cooks or servants. Then, in 1865, as construction of the transcontinental railroad got underway, 15,000 to 20,000 Chinese men found work on the tracks. Immigration continued, and, by 1880, some 100,000 Chinese men and 3,000 Chinese women had made their way to the west coast.

However, the Chinese were not welcomed with open arms, mainly because it was believed they were taking jobs, albeit low-paying ones, away from white Americans. In response to that concern, Congress passed the 1882 Chinese Exclusion Act, a law that prevented virtually all immigration from China to the United States. It was not overturned until 1943 when China joined the Allies during World War II. Even then, only 103 Chinese were

A view of Doyers Street as one approaches the bloody angle (circa 1909). (Bain Collection, Library of Congress Prints and Photographs Division)

allowed to immigrate each year, a number so small that it seems ridiculously silly. It wasn't until passage of the 1965 Immigration and Nationality Act that Chinese were able to operate under the same immigration rules as everyone else.

Manhattan in the mid-1800s had only a small population of Chinese, mostly merchants and sailors. That began to change in 1869 when the transcontinental railroad was completed and all the workers were let go. Many of those now unemployed Chinese men headed east to New York City in search of a new way to make a living. Most could only afford to live in the lowest of the low-rent districts. In Manhattan at that time, that included the old, creaky tenement buildings of Mott Street, Pell Street, and Doyers Street, most of them recently abandoned by the Irish and Jewish communities. Soon, Chinese shops and stores occupied the lower floors, while opium dens and gambling houses offering the games of Fan-Tan and Pai Gow moved into the upper stories. Manhattan now had its Chinatown.

In 1899, there was a movement led by James Jay Coogan, President of the Borough of Manhattan, to tear down many of the old Chinatown buildings and widen the streets. On March 16, at a hearing of the Board of Local Improvements of the Tenth District, Reverend Dr. McLoughlin, rector of the nearby Roman Catholic Church of the Transfiguration, spoke in favor of the changes. To say this man of the cloth did not like either the Chinese or Doyers Street would be an understatement. Here is some of what he said the next day, as reported by *The Brooklyn Citizen*:

"Those who have at heart the physical welfare of a community are agreed that the greatest promoters of health are sunshine and fresh air, and that the greatest barriers to health are narrow streets and alleys where the poor people crowd together, where the sun seldom shines, where the air is stifling, and where the filth is unmentionable. In all New York City there is not a more disagreeable street than Pell Street, nor a more forbidding cowpath than Doyers Street. If there must be a Chinese quarter, let it be large and airy, where the citizens of our great metropolis may have room to walk in the middle of the street without being compelled to come in contact with those aliens whom our government so despises that it will not grant them the right of citizenship.

"I come here as the Catholic pastor of a large congregation. I live in the midst of Chinatown. I am kept awake night after night in the summertime by the noise of these Mongolians, by their vile music, by the clatter of their tongues, by their dominoes, their unauthorized midnight processions, and by the shrill laughter of their white women. Hence I know fully whereof I speak when I pronounce Pell and Doyers Streets cesspools of immorality vile enough to bring a curse upon the entire community."

Despite these views, the transformation of Chinatown never materialized, and most of those buildings remain standing today.

For many at the bottom rung of the economic ladder, the best hope for survival meant turning to crime. From the beginning, Chinatown was dominated by several gangs. By far the two most powerful and enduring were the Hip Sing Tong and the On Leong Tong.

The Hip Sing were formed in San Francisco in the 1890s and expanded to Manhattan's Chinatown by the turn of the century. Eventually, the tong added chapters in several other cities, including Chicago, Boston, Philadelphia, and Seattle. The On Leong were a homegrown gang, first appearing in New York's Chinatown in 1893.

Most of the time the two gangs maintained an uneasy truce, with each side staying on their own turf. The Hip Sing had their headquarters on Pell Street, the On Leong on Mott. But every few years, a disagreement of some sort would kick-start a new war, prompting a period of flashing knives and bullets ripping through the neighborhood, and stone-cold dead victims showing up on the streets and in the dark halls and backrooms of tenement buildings.

The Chinese Opera house on Doyer Street was built in 1893, but by the early 1900's it was better known as the Chinese Theater. It was the setting for one of the deadliest battles between two notorious Chinese gangs. (Photo from Bain Collection, Library of Congress Prints and Photographs Division)

A war could last anywhere from a few days to a few years before the tong's hierarchies would figure out a way to arrange a truce and things would settle down for a time.

One of the deadliest battles between the two gangs took place on the night of Sunday, August 5, 1905, in a theater at 5–7 Doyers Street. The theater, called the Chinese Opera House, had been built in 1893 and was the first Chinese-language theater in the east. Straight-back benches provided seating for about 500 theatergoers. By 1905, it was more commonly known as the Chinese Theater and the popular venue attracted Asians and non-Asians as well. Sunday though, was visiting day in Chinatown for Chinese from other parts of New York and New Jersey. On Sunday nights, the theater was always mostly Chinese.

There was a long-standing unwritten rule among the gangs that the Chinese Theater was neutral ground. Hip Sings and On Leongs could go there, staying comfortably apart, and all would enjoy a night of entertainment. This all changed that Sunday. The Hip Sings were unhappy that some On Leongs had testified against them in a recent gambling case. And they were going to extract revenge, even if it meant breaking that unwritten rule.

The play that night was a popular one at the time, "The King's Daughter," and the theater was full. About 10 p.m., midway through the performance, a member of the Hip Sings reportedly lit a string of firecrackers and tossed them on or near the stage. As the popping firecrackers sent everyone into a panic, Hip Sings pulled out revolvers and started shooting at On Leongs. The On Leongs immediately fired back. Screams and smoke filled the air, and blood began to flow.

The battle ended when police arrived minutes later and the theater quickly cleared out. A reporter describing the scene wrote: "the police found four men unconscious on the floor. The seats, curtains, and scenery were riddled with lead. The floor was littered with pigtails, pistols, hats, coats, and debris which had been shot from the ceiling and walls. In this pile lay the four unconscious men."

All four died, two of them residents of Doyers Street. Some 20 people were wounded, although it seems remarkable, considering the circumstances, that this number wasn't higher. As the smoke cleared, everyone understood that a new tong war was about to get underway in Chinatown.

The wars between the Hip Sings and the On Leongs continued on and off until the Great Depression. By 1931, one in four Chinese men were out of work and the police started cracking down on gambling in Chinatown. Meanwhile, the build-up to World War II was beginning. All this meant the tong wars in Chinatown were all but done, giving way to the ferocious battles fought on distant shores by the Allied forces in Europe and the Pacific. More than 20,000 Chinese-Americans fought in the war, many of them from Manhattan's Chinatown.

When the Chinese Theater closed in 1911, the space became home to the Doyers Street Rescue Society or, as it was sometimes called, the Doyers Street Midnight Mission. It served Chinatown's homeless and destitute for the next 25 years.

No obvious evidence of the old theater or the mission remains today. Instead, at 5 Doyers Street, you'll find a 120-seat restaurant called the Chinese Tuxedo, a trendy eatery that attracts diners from all over the city. The fare includes dishes like shrimp and lobster

A shoeshine boy sits in front of The Doyers Street Rescue Society (circa 1930). The Rescue Society moved into the location when the Chinese Theater closed for good in 1911. (Photo by Irving Browning/Browning Photograph Collection, The New York Historical Society)

toast with chili and conpoy jam; hot and sour steak tartare with crab crackers; roasted duck breast; and basil and lychees with plum dressing.

In addition to the Chinese Tuxedo, there are several other Chinese restaurants along the street, the most well-known of which is the Nom Wah Tea Parlor, a place that, according to its website, opened at 13–15 Doyers in 1920 before moving to its current location at 13 Doyers Street (see page 128).

Thankfully, the "bloody angle" is bloody no more – unless you count the Bloody Marys that jump-start a good many of the brunches served in the neighborhood's restaurants. And don't panic if you hear footsteps approaching you quickly from behind. They won't be those of a gang member but, more likely, a busy investment advisor hurrying to meet a client. The meeting will include some gambling, but the risk will only involve how much money to put into the stock market.

The Nom Wah Tea Parlor

It's New York's oldest continuously operating dim sum joint.

Original location: 13–15 Doyers Street
Current location: 13 Doyers Street
Nearest subway stop: Canal Street Station/Centre Street

....

Dim Sum is a Chinese meal, usually served with tea, comprising a variety of small plates that include dumplings and other snack dishes. Diners typically pick and choose from several options to make a meal, either the traditional way – from carts pushed around the dining room by waitstaff – or, in some restaurants more recently, from a printed menu. Either way, everyone at the table gets to enjoy a tasty dinner made up of an assortment of dishes.

It's believed dim sum got its game on some 2,000 years ago when traders in the far east began traveling the silk roads. Travelers on those roads (they were actually more often narrow paths) needed food and rest on their journeys, so tea houses sprang up along the way. In addition to tea, travelers were offered dim sum as a meal.

Today, throughout the five boroughs of New York City – especially Manhattan, Queens, and Brooklyn – there are dozens of dim sum restaurants from which to choose. But the grandaddy of them all is the Nom Wah Tea Parlor, a bandbox of a place located at the "bloody angle" on Doyers Street in Manhattan's Chinatown.

According to Nom Wah's website, the restaurant opened at 13–15 Doyers Street in 1920 and back then it operated mainly as a bakery. The website goes on to say that Nom Wah's specialty at the time was the traditional Chinese mooncake, a sweet confectionary filled with red bean and lotus paste. It was sold each fall on the days leading up to the annual Chinese mid-autumn festival. Nom Wah customers would line up out the door and along the sidewalk to buy them for the holiday.

Dim Sum was a minor item on the menu during those early days at Nom Wah. Gradually, however, as more diners developed a yearning for it, Nom Wah became less known for its bakery and more known for its dim sum.

Nom Wah Tea Parlor, circa 1955. (Anthony Angel Collection, Library of Congress, Prints & Photographs Division)

No one seems to know who originally owned the restaurant. At some point, Edward Choy and his wife May became the owners of both the Nom Wah Tea Parlor at 13 Doyers Street and the Nom Wah Bakery Company next door at 15 Doyers. The earliest record I could find of the two Nom Wah businesses was in the 1940 Manhattan City Directory.

A *New York Times* article dated November 7, 1945, reported that the tea parlor at 13 Doyers had been operating since 1937 and the bakery at 15 Doyers since 1932. At some point the Choys ended the bakery operation, although as late as 1959 the bakery was still operating as the Nom Wah Co., Inc.

The Choys continued to own and operate the tea parlor until they lost the lease in 1968. No big deal for them, though. They simply moved the place next door to where the bakery was at 13 Doyers Street. And that's where you'll find the Nom Wah Tea Parlor today.

In 1974, when both Edward and May Choy were about 58 years old, they sold the Tea Parlor to a nephew, Wally Tang. Mr. Tang had been working for Nom Wah since 1950, when he was just 16 years old. He continued to run the place until 2010 when he decided to retire and sell the restaurant to his 23-year-old nephew Wilson Tang.

Old New York buildings often have interesting histories. The building at 13 and 15 Doyers is certainly one of them. In 1890, it was occupied by a business called the Sheet Metal Machine Company. Before the year was over, all their assets were sold. In 1894, it was reported that one man was injured when fire broke out at a Chinese restaurant owned by the Ching Kee Company on the ground floor of 15 Doyers. In 1899, a man by the name of Chin

Jin opened a restaurant at 15 Doyers. He committed suicide three months later because the business was a financial failure.

By 1901, 13 Doyers Street was home to a carpenter's shop. A newspaper photo at the time shows a carpenter named Lee Young standing in front of his shop at this location, with the façade of the building decorated in mourning for the recent death of President McKinley.

According to an article that ran in the *Brooklyn Daily Eagle* in March 1908, a new restaurant called the Mandarin Tea Garden opened at 11–13 Doyers Street a few years later. An article out of New York that ran in the *Kansas City Star* mentioned the new Mandarin Tea Garden served tea, dim sum and other Chinese dishes. The Mandarin Tea Garden was still there in 1922, according to an article in the *New York Tribune* dated October 1 of that year.

In 1910, the building next door at 15–17 Doyers was partially damaged when a fire broke out on the second story in the kitchen of the Yet Lok Wing restaurant. Three people died but fortunately nearly 200 tenants in the building managed to escape. The entire six-story building was burned out, although the walls and roof were saved.

Chinese gangs went at each other with regularity on Doyers Street back then. In 1925, Gee Ung, a member of the Hip Sing tong, was shot to death in a hallway at 15–17 Doyers. That same year, Hauk Kee, a member of rival gang the On Leong tong, was shot to death in the basement of the Hin Yung Restaurant at 15 Doyers Street. Lee Moy, owner of the restaurant, decided to retire after the killing.

In 1939, the building at 11–13 Doyers suffered damage from another fire that started next door at 15–17 Doyers. Seven people died at the 15–17 address. Later that same year, because of the fire

The Nom Wah Tea Parlor as it looks today. (Photo by author)

damage, both buildings were partially demolished. Two stories at 11–13 and four stories at 15–17 were removed, resulting in both buildings ending up two stories high. It's not clear how the two Nom Wah businesses adjusted to the upheaval caused by this fire.

Today, though, under the ownership of Wilson Tang, the Nom Wah Tea Parlor is going stronger than ever. He has modernized the kitchen yet managed to maintain the look and feel of the original dining room. So, if the urge for Dim Sum strikes you as you stroll along Doyers Street, get yourself a table at Nom Wah. Then, after you get comfortably seated, take a moment to look around appreciate the history of the restaurant and the building itself. Both are tightly woven into the remarkable fabric of Chinatown's past.

The Brooklyn Bridge Pedestrian Stampede

In 1883, only a week after the bridge opened, 12 people were crushed to death and dozens injured when panic set in on the crowded pedestrian walkway.

Location: New York side of the Brooklyn Bridge walkway
Nearest subway stop: Brooklyn Bridge – City Hall Station/Chambers Street

....

When the East River Bridge opened to enormous fanfare on Thursday, May 24, 1883, many called it the Eighth Wonder of the World. Years later, the grand structure would become better known by the name we now use – the Brooklyn Bridge.

The deck of the bridge today looks much different than back then. Although the roughly mile-long pedestrian walkway – sometimes called the "promenade" – is still in the center lane, the bridge originally had two trolley tracks, one on each side of the walkway. And on each side of the trolley track was a relatively narrow lane for horse-drawn carriages and wagons; one to carry eastbound traffic, the other for westbound traffic. Nowadays, each side of the walkway has a three-lane road, with one road going eastbound, the other road going westbound. No trucks are allowed.

Brooklyn Bridge with lower Manhattan in the background, circa 1915. (Library of Congress, Prints & Photographs Division)

In a typical year, the bridge carries an average of 116,000 vehicles, 30,000 pedestrians, and 3,000 cyclists each day.

Originally, the pedestrian walkway was 18 ft. wide and mostly straight and flat. But at the point where the four drooping 16 in. diameter cables extended from the towers to below the bridge deck, the walkway was reduced to 15 ft. so it could squeeze between the two inside cables. This point also had another feature: in order to accommodate the change in elevation of the deck, there was a wooden stairway consisting of six lower steps, followed by a 7-foot-wide landing, then by seven more steps to the top. A pedestrian going up the staircase while walking from Manhattan to Brooklyn would gain about 9 ft. in elevation.

Six days after the bridge opening, Wednesday, May 30th, was Decoration Day, a holiday established to remember and honor the soldiers who died in the Civil War. For many New Yorkers, it would be the perfect holiday to take a stroll on the remarkable new bridge. For others, it was an opportunity to visit and decorate (hence the name) the graves of not only veterans but also family members who were buried in Brooklyn cemeteries across the river from Manhattan.

The day started with a few light rain showers, which made morning pedestrian traffic relatively light. But the sky cleared as the day progressed and the foot traffic began to grow. Over the course of the day, the pedestrian toll-booth records (pedestrians had to pay a penny to cross) showed that 55,974 men, women, and children entered the bridge from the New York side and another 41,250 came from the Brooklyn side.

By about 4 p.m. the foot traffic had become very heavy. Pedestrians moving from the New York side came up against a good many more pedestrians from the Brooklyn side as New Yorkers were returning to Manhattan. The two opposing forces began to jam together where the promenade narrowed at the staircase and soon that point became tightly packed. Some pushing and jostling, most of it unavoidable, started to occur. The crowd at the staircase began to get uncomfortable. That's when things started to go wrong.

A woman, described as middle aged and walking toward the New York side, tripped while going down the stairs and fell on the landing. This caused another woman to scream, which in turn prompted the crowd moving toward New York to push forward to see what the commotion was all about. Perhaps prompted by the confusion, someone was said to have yelled that the bridge was about to collapse.

Here's some of what was reported in *The New York Times* two days later:

Those on the promenade above the stairway, knowing nothing of the fearful crush on the steps, surged ahead with irresistible force, and in a moment the whole stairway was packed with dead and dying men, women and children piled one upon another in a writhing, struggling mass.

The New York Sun reported:

The first to be lifted out was a boy perhaps 10 years of age. His face had been trampled to a pulp and, so far as I could judge, he was dead. A young woman, almost nude, was laid on the drive and died almost instantly. A young woman with a broken rib protruding through her breast, was carried across the track. She seemed to be lifeless. The scene before the victims were carried away was sad in the extreme. Dead and wounded were lying close together on the roadways and against the stone railings. Kind hands made the positions of the wounded as comfortable as possible, but the moans and groans which filled the air made strong men weep . . . Hats went over into the railroad tracks and fell to the housetops and streets below in showers. Canes and umbrellas were broken, shawls were torn from womens' shoulders and veils from their faces and trampled underfoot.

Police eventually managed to pushed the crowd back and gain some control, and it was all over in just a few minutes. In that time, 12 people died and dozens were taken to local hospitals. Many more who suffered injuries no doubt went home and relied on the family medicine cabinet to take care of minor cuts and scrapes.

A few days later, on June 6th, a coroner's jury inquest was held. After hearing from those questioned, and then deliberating for about an hour, the jurors announced their verdict:

We find the Trustees and officers reprehensible in not having the bridges and its approaches properly policed, and particularly at the steps. Had this important matter received the careful attention of the managers of the bridge to which it was intitled, the vast throng upon the structure would have been kept moving and the panic, which resulted in the deaths of 12 persons, averted; and that the construction of the footway and steps is not of sufficient capacity for the accommodations of the foot passengers.

The jurors went on to say that the bridge Trustees had to "give their serious attention to making sure the promenade was absolutely safe." Additional police were immediately assigned to the bridge with instructions to keep a close eye on foot traffic at the stairway. The extra police, and a gradual reduction in foot traffic over time as the novelty of the bridge promenade began to diminish, have managed to keep the bridge safe from such an event since that day.

These days the bridge is rarely crowded. But rarely doesn't mean never. For example, on December 29, 2018, the bridge encountered heavy foot traffic thanks to an unusually balmy 50-degree day and a flood of Christmas-holiday tourists. It prompted the office of New York mayor Bill de Blasio to tweet: "The Brooklyn Bridge is very crowded at the moment. While this is not an emergency situation, please exercise caution if you are on the bridge and expect long wait times if you intend to visit this afternoon."

The site of the stampede today. The staircase is no longer there; it was removed after the incident. (Photo by author)

At least a few people on the bridge felt less comfortable with what they were seeing firsthand. One person tweeted: "Pedestrian Traffic Jam. Overcapacity on Brooklyn Bridge. Stuck for 40 minutes." Another said: "Stuck on the Brooklyn Bridge pedestrian walk for an hour now. Very overcrowded." And yet another tweeted ominously: "The Brooklyn Bridge ped path is dangerously overcrowded right now. People are pushing and yelling. NYPD is sitting in their little three-wheelers doing nothing about crowd control. It's a mess. Stampede waiting to happen. Worst I've ever seen." Fortunately, no one panicked that day and everyone got off the bridge without incident.

The staircase was removed many years ago and the walkway leading to it was made into a long, gradual uphill grade that gets pedestrians to the needed elevation without much exertion. No part of the staircase remains today. But you can find its former location if you stand at the point on the Manhattan side of the bridge where the walkway narrows to allow the two inner cables to reach below the deck.

America's first pizza joint

The Italian tomato pie got its New World start in Manhattan.

Location: 192 Grand Street
Nearest subway stop: Spring Street Station at Lafayette Street

....

It would be a wild understatement to say that Americans like pizza. We don't simply like pizza; we are head over heels in love with it.

Testament to that love can be found in the roughly 77,000 mom-and-pop and chain pizza restaurants found across the United States; from Portland, Maine to Portland, Oregon, from Columbus, Texas to Columbus, Ohio. And, each year, Americans affirm that profound affection for pizza by eating, on average, 46 slices of it. That's a lot of amore.

The pizza we enjoy today has roots tracing back at least 2,000 years to the simple flatbreads common to Persia and Europe. No doubt, at some point, an adventurous eater decided to add a topping or two, back then most likely lard or olive oil or olives or cheese.

Pizza saw a big evolutionary jump in the sixteenth century after the tomato plant was brought to Europe, probably from Central or South America or perhaps Mexico. Residents of Naples, Italy, and the surrounding region of Campania quickly took a liking to the never-seen-before fruit. It was both tasty and inexpensive and soon they were adding it to their flatbreads, along with cheese, olive oil, and herbs. By the eighteenth century, Naples was well known throughout Italy for its tomato pies.

By the mid-nineteenth century, prompted mostly by poverty, many Italians began to look beyond their shores for a better life. As a result, from the years 1861 to 1914, some 16 million Italians immigrated to the United States, many from southern Italian cities like Naples. And with them came their love of pizza – and the skill to make it.

One of those immigrants was Filippo Milone. Thanks to the work of Peter Regas, a dedicated pizza historian from Chicago,

Built in 1901, this place at 192 Grand Street was home in 1903 to Antica Pizzeria Port'Alba – the first known pizza joint in the United States. Today it's the location of a restaurant called Tomino. (Photo by author)

ANTICA PIZZERIA PORT'ALBA
Alias Port'a Seluscella
FILIPPO MILONE, Prop.
PIZZERIA NAPOLEANA aperta GIORNO E NOTTE
192 GRAND St., NEW YORK
Il conosciuto Proprietario dell'Antica Pizzeria Port'Alba, Signor FIILPPo MI-LONE, fa noto al Pubblico che ha aperto al N.o 192 Grand St., un'Elegante PIZ-ZERIA NAPOLETANA.
Essendo l unico locale Italiano del ge-nere, fa sperare al Signor FILIPPO MI-LONE il concorso numeroso di Italiani. Come pure fa noto al pubblico che quan to prima verrà annesso alla pizzeria una Cucina Casereccia per colezione alla For-chetta.
I buongustai vadano a mangiare le squi site PIZZE che fa il simpatico Filippo Milone nella sua Nuova Pizzeria al N.o 192 Grand St.

An advertisement from the May 9, 1903 issue of the Italian-language newspaper Il Telegrafo. (New York Public Library; image of advertisement scanned by author Peter Regas)

we know Milone came to New York from Naples in the 1890s. Regas also learned – from an advertisement he discovered in the Italian-American newspaper *Il Telegrafo* dated May 9, 1903 – that Milone owned and operated a pizza restaurant called Antica Pizzeria Port'Alba at 192 Grand Street in Manhattan. That makes Antica the first known pizza joint in the United States.

Before Regas spotted that newspaper ad, it was universally accepted that the oldest pizza restaurant in the United States was Lombardi's, opened in 1905 by Gennaro Lombardi at 52½ Spring Street in Little Italy. Lombardi's, now located at 32 Spring Street, continues to maintain that it's "America's first pizzeria."

Even though that claim has now been questioned, Lombardi's still holds a special place in the history of American pizza. Except for the decade between 1984 and 1994, they have been making their pies nonstop in Little Italy since the day they opened in 1905. That's an impressive run of pizza making.

142

It has been a long time since a bubbling-hot pizza came out of Antica Pizzeria Port'Alba's oven at 192 Grand Street. Today the address is home to a restaurant specializing in food from the Galicia region of Spain. However, thanks to Filippo Milone, the little joint he ran there at the turn of last century is for now fully baked into culinary history as the spot where Americans first fell forever in love with the glorious Italian disk of dough, tomato sauce, cheese, and toppings we call the pizza pie.

The Wall Street bombing

Pockmarks scattered across the limestone facade of the former J. P. Morgan Company headquarters are evidence of a bomb that exploded there in 1920, killing 38 people and injuring hundreds.

Location: 23 Wall Street
Nearest subway stop: Broad Street Station

....

The sky was overcast on Thursday, September 16, 1920, as the bells of Trinity Church peeled 12 times to announce the noon hour to anyone within earshot of Manhattan's financial district.

Two blocks away, at the intersection of Wall Street and Broad Street, the sidewalks outside the J.P. Morgan Company building were bustling with hundreds of pedestrians, most of them going about the business of doing Wall Street's business. Almost unnoticed to any passersby was a one-horse wagon that just minutes earlier had been left unattended across the street from the Morgan building and directly in front of the United States Assay Office at 30 Wall Street, next to what was then called the Sub-Treasury Building at 36 Wall Street (now the Federal Hall National Memorial).

No one could have guessed that the nondescript wagon was filled with 100 pounds of dynamite and an estimated 500 pounds of cast-iron sash weights, an item typically used to balance windows

Aftermath of the explosion (Library of Congress Prints and Photographs Division)

that have movable frames. The dynamite was there to generate explosive force. The sash-weights, each broken into two or three pieces, were there for killing and maiming. An attached timing device served as a means to trigger what newspaper reporters would later call the "infernal machine." At 12:01 p.m., the wagon exploded.

A nearby automobile was sent airborne by the explosion. Two blocks away, a trolley car was knocked off its tracks. A piece of shrapnel, still hot, landed on the deck of a ferry docked on the Hudson River at the Cortlandt Street Ferry Terminal, more than half a mile from the blast.

Bernard F. Kennedy was a 29-year-old clerk working at the brokerage firm Johnson and Wood on Broadway. During World

War I he'd seen 11 months' service in France as a private in the 77th Division, where he suffered through gas attacks and took a piece of German shrapnel in the knee. He died that day on Wall Street when a piece of the bomb shrapnel struck him in the head.

Ella Perry, a 22-year-old stenographer, was in her office at 36 Wall Street at the moment when the bomb went off. Immediately, she said, glass and ceiling plaster fell everywhere in the office. When she and some coworkers ran to the exit, police told them to stay back. "I looked down into the street and saw the reason. What I saw was awful. There were not less than a dozen dead persons on the sidewalk in front of our building and the Sub-Treasury. Some of them had their faces almost completely blown off and

Police placed the bodies of some victims along a sidewalk. (Library of Congress Prints and Photographs Division)

146

The pockmarked façade of
the J.P. Morgan building.
(Photo by author)

their clothing had either been blown from their bodies or burned off. The police threw sheets over the bodies as fast as they could get them."

According to the *New York Tribune*: "Not a sound pane of glass remained in the Morgan Building. The streets were covered with broken glass, some of it finely powdered, like sugar."

Michael Kerwin, a World War I veteran, was working as a clerk at a cigar store well within the blast zone. After the explosion, he ran out of the tattered store front looking for victims to help. He immediately came upon three unconscious men with their clothing burning. Using his knife, he managed to cut away their garments while at the same time beating at the flames until they were finally smothered. All three victims died a short time later.

If, as some speculated later, the plan was to target the barons of Wall Street – perhaps even J.P. Morgan, Jr. himself – the scheme was completely unsuccessful. Jack Morgan wasn't anywhere near the bank that day; he was in Europe. Junius Morgan, Jack's 28-year-old son, was in the building and suffered a cut on the hand.

Almost all of those killed were the grunts of Wall Street: clerks, runners, tellers, brokers, messengers, and stenographers. The youngest to die was 16-year-old Benjamin Soloway, a messenger; the oldest was 67-year-old Edwin Sweet, a retired banker. Five of the dead were women.

No one was ever arrested for the crime, although not for lack of effort. The police kept the case opened for 20 years. The most likely suspect was a 35-year-old anarchist born in Italy and living in Boston named Mario Buda. Investigators believed he was enraged because, just a few days earlier in Massachusetts, the anarchists Nicola Sacco and Bartolomeo Vanzetti, who Buda knew personally, were charged with killing two people while robbing a shoe-factory.

Buda went back to Italy a few days after the bombing and changed his name. Years later, in 1955, he allegedly admitted to his nephew that he had been responsible for the bombing that day. He died in Italy in 1963 at the age of 78.

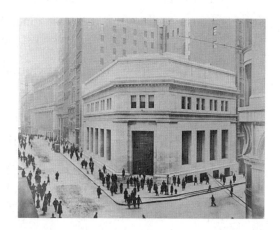

The J.P. Morgan building, circa 1915. (Library of Congress Prints and Photographs Division)

The J.P. Morgan building today. (Photo by author)

The bombing has now largely been forgotten. No memorial, monument, plaque, or even a hand-painted sign was ever erected to honor those who died. The scarred limestone façade of Jack Morgan's old building is the only visible marker we have, silently serving to remind us of what happened there many years ago.

Alexander Hamilton's grave

This youngest founding father helped shape the future of our brand-new country.

Location: The Churchyard at Trinity Church; Broadway and Wall Street
Nearest subway stop: Wall Street Station/Broadway

....

When Alexander Hamilton first appears in the opening act of Lin-Manuel Miranda's Broadway musical *Hamilton*, he announces:

> My name is Alexander Hamilton.
> And there's a million things I haven't done,
> but just you wait,
> just you wait . . .

No doubt he would have done more had he not died in 1804 at the age of 47 (or 49 – his birthdate is unclear) in a duel with Aaron Burr. Hamilton had been President George Washington's secretary of the treasury and, at the time of the duel, Burr was the sitting vice-president of the United States under the current president, Thomas Jefferson.

Hamilton's death stunned the young nation. As much as anyone back then, young Hamilton's efforts had made it possible for the fledgling republic to spread its wings and fly at a time when its

Alexander Hamilton, oil on canvas, by John Trumbull, 1806. (National Portrait Gallery, Smithsonian Institution; gift of Henry Cabot Lodge)

future was very much uncertain. As one writer said of him, "He, more than any other of our early statesmen, did the thinking of his time."

Hamilton was born on the tiny volcanic island of Nevis in the British West Indies. His father, James A. Hamilton, was a merchant from Scotland. His mother, Rachel Fawcett, was born in Nevis of French ancestry. The two never married. When Alexander was born, Rachel was still married to another man she had separated from several years earlier. A traditional family it was not.

In 1766, James moved Rachel, Alexander, and his younger brother James, Jr. to the nearby island of St. Croix. A short time later he abruptly left them. Within two years Rachel died of yellow fever. Alexander was 11 years old.

Relatives of Rachel living on St. Croix collected both orphaned boys and cared for them. In 1769, 12-year-old Alexander took a job as a clerk in a large mercantile store. His skill and intellect so impressed the owner of the business that a year later he put Alexander in charge of the entire store while he traveled to the American colonies.

When not working, Hamilton would often be found with his nose in a book, learning everything he could about the world beyond the West Indies. Two of his favorite authors were Plutarch and the English poet Alexander Pope. Hamilton's work and studies didn't go unnoticed. His employer soon arranged to send him to the American colonies so that he might obtain an education appropriate to his potential.

After a year of grammar school in New Jersey, in 1773 Hamilton entered King's College (now Columbia University), at the time located at the corner of Murray and Church Streets in lower Manhattan. While there he began to sympathize with and support the growing protests against the British government. At about the same time, he started drilling with a company of volunteer militiamen.

Hamilton left college in 1775 at the outbreak of the Revolutionary War and volunteered for military service where he was put in charge of an artillery battery. His intellect along with good measures of skill and courage in the field of battle caught the eye of his superiors, including General George Washington. At Washington's request, Hamilton became his military aide, more commonly called an aide-de-camp, with the rank of lieutenant colonel. He served in that position for four years.

In 1780, while still serving General Washington, he married Elizabeth (often called Eliza) Schuyler, the daughter of General Philip Schuyler of Albany, New York, a well-to-do and respected

King's College (later to become Columbia University), circa 1770, when it was located in lower Manhattan at the corner of Murray Street and Church Street. Hamilton attended the school in 1773. (Wikimedia Commons)

landowner who served with distinction in the Continental Army until 1779. Elizabeth and Alexander had eight children together, the first one born in 1782, the last one born in 1802.

After four years spent mostly sitting behind a desk in the field, Hamilton was getting itchy. He wanted to get back to active combat duty. Washington was cool to the idea, but after a good deal of prodding by Hamilton, he relented and gave him command of a battalion of light infantry companies. At the Battle of Yorktown in 1781, the actions of Hamilton and his troops were instrumental

Hamilton as a commander of a battalion of light infantry companies. (oil on canvas (1857) by Alonzo Chappel (Wikimedia Commons)

in securing a victory over the British, a battle that effectively ended the war.

Hamilton resigned his military commission in 1782 and soon began teaching himself everything he needed to know to get a law degree. He passed the bar exam later that year and established a practice in New York City. At about the same time he was elected to Congress – at the time called the Congress of the Confederation and located in Philadelphia – as a representative of New York.

He resigned from Congress in 1783, and, when the British evacuated New York City on November 25th of that year, Hamilton left Philadelphia with his family and moved back to New York to continue practicing law. Ironically, as a lawyer, he often took cases defending Tories and subjects of the British Crown who remained in the city. He also carved out time to found the Bank of New York.

While his ambitions were big, Hamilton's physical size has been described as on the smallish side. Author James Edward Graybill put him at 5 foot 6 inches tall and about 130 pounds. Another author, Edward S. Ellis in his 1898 biography, *Alexander Hamilton: A Character Sketch*, described Hamilton's physical appearance at that point in his life in this way:

> He was under the middle size, thin in person, and very erect, courtly and dignified in his bearing. His hair was combed back from his forehead, powdered and collected in a cue behind. His complexion was very delicate and fair, his cheeks rosy, and the whole expression pleasing and cheerful. His forehead was lofty, capacious and prominent, which his prodigious fame excited.

His voice was musical, his manner frank and impulsive. His ordinary dress was a blue coat with gilt buttons, a white silk waistcoat, black silk small-clothes, and white silk stockings.

In 1786, he was one of two delegates from New York invited to attend the Annapolis Convention in Maryland. The purpose of the convention, which was held at Mann's Tavern in Annapolis, was to give delegates from throughout the colonies an opportunity to discuss trade issues between the states. However, the original agenda soon gave way to talk focused on grievances related to the Articles of Confederation. As a result, what started out as a relatively obscure gathering in Maryland turned out to be the driving force to get Congress to call a Constitutional Convention.

Good to its word, Congress convened a Constitutional Convention in Philadelphia in 1787 with a goal to review and, where necessary, overhaul the Articles of Confederation. Benjamin Franklin recommended George Washington to preside over the goings-on and the war hero soon was elected president-general of the gathering. Hamilton was chosen to attend as one of three delegates from New York State.

At the time, long speeches by politicians were not uncommon. However, at that convention, Hamilton raised the bar for speech-length to a new level – six hours – reportedly speaking without notes the entire time. Clearly, this was a man with stronger than average convictions. He spent most of the marathon oration imploring other delegates to establish a stronger central government.

Hamilton's concern about a weak central government was not completely unfounded. At the time, the United States was little more than a collection of 13 individual nations loosely bound by the Articles of Confederation that gave scant power to the federal government. Indeed, the collective 13 states, George Washington reportedly said, "were held together by little more than a rope of sand."

As a result, Congress couldn't do basic tasks like collect taxes, conduct foreign policy, establish a singular national currency (individual states minted their own coins), or raise a national army (state militias handled national defense). Also, because Congress couldn't establish a national court system, states often ignored national laws because there was nothing Congress could do to enforce them. Hamilton wanted to change all that and give much more power to a central government. Without such changes, he felt, the new country would be forever unable to achieve the lofty goals set forth in the Declaration of Independence.

As it turned out, the delegates at the Philadelphia convention did much more than review the Articles of Confederation. They spent four months, much of it in the stifling summer heat in Independence Hall (where, 11 years earlier, the Declaration of Independence was signed), hammering into shape a brand-new constitution, one with a much stronger federal government to do the heavy lifting. In September of 1787, the new constitution was sent to the 13 states for ratification. Adoption of the document, however, was far from a sure thing.

Hamilton, John Jay, and James Madison argued for passage of the new constitution by writing some 85 essays directed mainly at the New York State delegation. Hamilton penned 51 of them. The essays came to be called The Federalist Papers and caused quite a stir when published piecemeal in a few New York newspapers during a six-month period between October 1787 and April 1788.

New York State ultimately voted for ratification, but the vote occurred after the Constitution had already been approved by nine other states, the number that was needed to make it official. In the grand scheme of things, The Federalist Papers had little effect on the ultimate ratification of the Constitution. However, to this day they are regularly read, studied, and considered invaluable by academics, legislators, and courts as a way to try and understand and interpret the original intent of the writers of the Constitution.

Washington was inaugurated President of the United States on April 16, 1789, taking the oath of office at Federal Hall in New York City. The new president hadn't forgotten his young, talented aide-de-camp and soon named Hamilton as the first Secretary of the Treasury. Hamilton took office in September 1789, serving there for more than four years.

Hamilton raised the finances needed to pay various war debts through excise taxes and custom duties. But his efforts to make the United States financially sound were just getting started. He created the first national bank, calling it the Bank of the United States. He worked to establish the United States Mint. He pushed policies that benefited not just farming, but also manufacturing, a segment of the economy existing mainly in the northeast and mostly ignored by the farming states. In 1790, Hamilton created the U.S. Revenue Cutter Service that put to use sleek, fast, armed ships, called cutters, to enforce custom regulations on the open sea. The organization later morphed into the U.S. Coast Guard.

Not everyone was head over heels for Hamilton's policies. No less than Thomas Jefferson and James Madison opposed him at just about every step, arguing that the new policies gave too much power to the federal government. The disagreements led to Hamilton organizing the Federalist Party – the first political party in the United States. Two years later, to counter the Federalists, Jefferson and Madison formed the Democratic-Republican Party (no direct relation to either of the today's main political parties in the United States).

The year 1792 saw Hamilton do more than start a political party – he also started an affair with a 23-year-old woman. Her name was Maria Reynolds, and she had approached him at his home in Philadelphia asking for financial help. She and her young daughter needed to get to friends in New York after her abusive husband had left her for another woman. It wasn't long before Maria's husband found out about the goings-on and demanded hush money. Hamilton paid him off and then ended the relationship. But a story like this is not easy to keep under wraps and soon it was public knowledge. Some of the details even suggested that Hamilton was also involved in an illegal speculation scheme involving Maria's former husband.

Hamilton decided the best way to deal with the crisis was to come clean. In 1897, he published a pamphlet describing the entire affair, blackmail details included, but denied having anything to do with illegal speculation. The pamphlet helped clear his name on this count, but his affair with a married woman ended any hope he likely had of becoming president. Through it all, Hamilton's wife Elizabeth, though painfully humiliated, stayed with him.

The arrival of the year 1798 found France and England at war. When France began seizing American ships that were trading with England, the United States and France faced off in an undeclared war called the Quasi-War. Most of the fighting took place at sea off the eastern coast of the United States and the Caribbean Islands.

Concerns that the Quasi-War might escalate to an all-out declared war led to the formation of a United States Provisional Army that would stand alongside the established United States Army. George Washington was coaxed out of retirement by President Adams and named commander-in-chief of the combined armies, with the understanding that Washington would remain at his home in Mt. Vernon unless the war got really hot. Needing someone in Philadelphia to take care of the day-to-day details of the complex job, it was no surprise that Washington appointed Hamilton as his number two man, making him Inspector General with a rank of major-general.

When George Washington died in late 1799, Hamilton was promoted to be the Army's senior officer. That meant he was now the commander-in-chief of the entire United States Army. The orphaned kid from the Caribbean was managing to do alright for himself in his adopted country.

By early 1800, thanks to diplomatic efforts by President John Adams that Hamilton opposed, the Quasi-War was winding down. Adams had the provisional army disbanded on June 15, 1800 and Hamilton resigned as inspector general on the same day. The war officially ended when a peace treaty was signed between the United States and France on September 30, 1800.

Then, on February 17, 1801, Thomas Jefferson, a member of the Democratic-Republican Party, was elected President of the United States, effectively putting an end to Hamilton's Federalist Party. Aaron Burr was elected vice-president. Hamilton was now a private citizen, but he continued to influence public opinion through his writings and speeches. He also set about convincing private investors to help him launch a newspaper called *The New York Evening Post*. The first issue came off the presses in November 1801. Now he had his own newspaper. And with it came a big soapbox to use against political opponents. The newspaper is still published today as the *New York Post*, and it has the distinction of being the oldest continuously published newspaper in the United States.

The year 1801 also brought a stunning tragedy to the Hamilton family. On November 24, 19-year-old Philip Hamilton, the oldest son of Alexander and Elizabeth, was killed in a duel. The death devastated the Hamilton family. A friend of Alexander's wrote at the time, "Never did I see a man so completely overwhelmed with grief as Hamilton has been." It caused Philip's 17-year-old sister, Angelica, to suffer a mental breakdown from which she never recovered. She required special care until she died in 1847 at the age of 72.

Philip's death caused an instant change in Hamilton. He spent less time on affairs of state and more time focusing on his family and law practice in New York. Part of that time was spent overseeing the construction of a new country house for Eliza and the children. It was built on 32 acres of mostly open farmland in Harlem, about 10 miles north of his law office in the city. It was the only house Alexander and Eliza ever owned, and getting there required a 90-minute journey by horse-carriage. He named it "The Grange" after the parish in Stevenson, Scotland, where Hamilton's father had roots going back to the 1500s.

The Federal-style two-story, wood-framed house was designed by John McComb, Jr., an A-list architect with a body of work that

The Grange, the house Hamilton built in 1802 and the only place he ever owned. It is shown here in its original location. After his death in 1804, his wife Elizabeth continued to live there until about 1834 when she sold the house for $25,000. The house was then moved twice, first in 1889 and then again in 2006. (National Park Service)

included Gracie Mansion and New York City Hall. As part of the landscaping, Hamilton planted 13 sweetgum trees in a circle in front of the house to represent the 13 original states. The family moved into the house in 1802.

The Grange still stands, although it has been moved twice over the years. It was originally located at what is now West 143rd Street and Convent Avenue. The house currently sits in St. Nicholas Park at West 141st Street and St. Nicholas Avenue, about 750 feet due south of its original location. The National Park Service owns the house and has designated it a national memorial site.

As the year 1804 arrived, Hamilton and his family were no doubt comfortably settled in the new house and enjoying the quiet and fresh air of country life. For Alexander, however, the business of politics was never very far from his mind. The Federalist Party he had worked hard to create was floundering, while the opposition – the Democratic-Republican Party – was solidly in power.

In February, the Democratic-Republican Party caucus met to finalize the ticket for the 1804 election. As expected, they chose President Thomas Jefferson to run for reelection. But the party had concerns about the loyalty of the current vice-president, Aaron Burr. As a result, Burr was dropped from the party ticket and replaced with George Clinton, the sitting governor of New York State.

Burr, a citizen of New York State, then decided to run for the open governor's seat against Morgan Lewis. Both Burr and Lewis

The Grange as it looks today in Manhattan's St. Nicholas Park. The house has been restored to its original glory by the National Park Service and it is open to the public. (National Park Service)

ran as Democratic-Republicans, but the two candidates represented different factions of the party. The election was held in April and Burr lost. He put much of the blame for his loss on Hamilton's rhetoric that was leveled against him during the campaign.

There had for a long time been bad political blood between Aaron Burr and Alexander Hamilton, going back to the Constitutional debates in 1789. In 1791, Burr got further under his skin when he ran against and defeated Hamilton's father-in-law, Philip Schuyler, for the U.S. Senate in 1791. Hamilton said at the time, "I fear (Aaron Burr) is unprincipled both as a public and private man." A year later he wrote, "I feel it a religious duty to oppose his career."

In the spring of 1804, as Burr's gubernatorial campaign was in full swing, Hamilton happened to visit a friend in Albany. While there he attended a dinner party at which candidate Burr's name came up. Hamilton reportedly used some unflattering terms when speaking about Burr. Some of his words ended up being printed in a local newspaper. When Burr saw the story months later, there was one comment in particular that stuck in his craw. The story claimed Hamilton said he had a "despicable" opinion of Burr. At that point, Burr immediately wrote to Hamilton asking for an explanation. A series of letters went back and forth, but the issue remained unresolved. In the end, Burr insisted that there was only one solution to the perceived affront – a duel.

The practice of dueling, usually with pistols, although sometimes with swords, was not uncommon in nineteenth-century America. Indeed, the United States Navy reported that between 1798 and 1861, about two-thirds as many officers died from dueling as from combat at sea. Any gentleman who perceived an offence could insist on a duel. To refuse was to be forever labeled a coward. Although illegal in New York and New Jersey, duels were quietly arranged in secluded places and euphemistically referred to as "interviews."

Hamilton and Burr met shortly after sunrise on Wednesday, July 11, 1804, in Weehawken, New Jersey, a favorite dueling ground for New Yorkers just across the Hudson River from New York and the same location where Hamilton's son Philip had dueled and died just two years earlier.

The two were rowed to the Jersey shore in separate boats. Each of them brought along an assistant, called a "second," to load the guns and make sure all the established rules of dueling were properly followed. Hamilton also brought along a doctor, a family friend, who stayed at the boat with the oarsmen. Here's how the two seconds described the encounter in a joint statement they made a few days later:

> "Colonel Burr arrived first on the ground, as had been previously agreed; when General Hamilton arrived the parties exchanged salutations, and the seconds proceeded to make their arrangements. They measured the distance, ten full paces, and cast lots for the choice of positions, as also to determine by whom the word should be given, both of which fell to the second of General Hamilton.
>
> "They then proceeded to load the pistols in each other's presence, after which the parties took their stations. He then asked if they were prepared; being answered in the affirmative, he gave the word 'Present,' as had been agreed on, and both parties presented and fired in succession – the intervening time is not expressed, as the seconds do not precisely agree on that point.

"The fire of Colonel Burr took effect, and General Hamilton almost instantly fell. Colonel Burr then advanced toward General Hamilton, with a manner and gesture that appeared to General Hamilton's friend to be expressive of regret, but without speaking, turned about and withdrew, being urged from the field by his friend, as has been subsequently stated, with a view to prevent his being recognized by the surgeon and bargemen, who were then approaching.

"No further communication took place between the principals, and the barge that carried Colonel Burr immediately returned to the city. We conceive it proper to add that the conduct of the parties in this interview was perfectly proper, as suited the occasion."

Hamilton's final resting place in the churchyard at Trinity Church; Broadway and Wall Street. (Photo by author)

Hamilton was alive but understood the shot was almost certainly fatal. Once back on the New York shore, he was brought by carriage to the nearby house of a friend.

He died there in the company of his wife and children, clergy, and friends about 2 p.m. the next day. His body was then moved to the home of his sister Angelica and her husband John Church on Park Place in lower Manhattan.

The funeral was held on Saturday July 14th, beginning with a long procession to the graveyard. Thousands of mourners lined the streets along the way. Flags were at half-staff. Newspapers framed their pages with black borders. In the harbor, American, British, and French frigates fired cannons in one-minute intervals as the procession wound its way to the churchyard.

A monument was later erected at the site. The epitaph carved into the stone reads:

The Patriot of incorruptible integrity.
The soldier of approved valour.
The statesman of consummate wisdom.
Whose talents and virtues will be admired
Long after this marble shall have mouldered into dust.

The recording studio
Jimi Hendrix built

He cut only one record there before he died in 1970, but the studio still survives today – and the artists who have since made music in the place read like a list of rock and roll all-stars.

Location: 52 West 8th Street
Nearest subway stop: West 4th Street/Washington Square

....

When *Rolling Stone* magazine published their take on the world's 100 greatest guitarists of all time, it was Jimi Hendrix who topped the list. That's not surprising. Unlike anyone before him, Hendrix could make the electric guitar do things that bordered on supernatural.

His playing was loud and fast and seemingly effortless. He'd force sounds from the instrument that no one had heard before. He'd play it behind his back just because he could. He'd play it with his teeth. And, sometimes, at the end of a performance, he'd smash his guitar to splinters or set it on fire with lighter fluid. Anyone fortunate enough to be at one of his performances would come away feeling like they had absorbed the energy and brightness of the sun itself.

Johnny Allen Hendrix was born in Seattle, Washington, on November 27, 1942, to 43-year-old James Marshall Hendrix, who everyone called Al, and 17- year-old Lucille Jeter. About four years later the parents renamed the boy James Marshal Hendrix to honor both Al and Al's brother, Leon Marshall, who died of a ruptured appendix earlier that same year.

It was not an idyllic childhood for young James, Al struggled to find work and Lucille had a drinking problem. They battled each other almost all the time and were often separated. She died of alcohol abuse in 1958 aged just 32.

Growing up, young James seemed to be obsessed with the guitar to the point that he was often seen strumming on the straw head of a broom. It wasn't until 1957, when he was 15 years old, that he got his hands on his first "instrument" — an old ukulele with just

Hendrix performing at the Gröna Lund Amusement Park in Stockholm, Sweden, May 24, 1967. (Wikimedia Commons)

one string. For someone obsessed with the guitar, though, a one-stringed ukulele was good enough. Soon he was plunking along to Elvis Presley's hit song "Hound Dog."

A year later, his father got him a real guitar, an acoustic. He then joined his first band, The Velvetones, in the summer of 1958. When James realized his acoustic guitar could barely be heard above the others in the band, Al got him an electric guitar. James took to it like a duck to water.

The Velvetones morphed into a short-lived group called The Rocking Teens, which soon begot The Rocking Kings in the summer of 1959. A year later, James and a few members of The Rocking Kings put together yet another new band – Thomas and the Tom Cats. The band was doing well enough that Hendrix quit high school before graduation and took on odd jobs so he could continue doing what he loved most – play the guitar and then play it some more.

In May 1961 he was arrested on two occasions for riding in stolen cars. Standing before a judge in juvenile court on May 16, 1961, Hendrix was told he had two choices; a two-year jail sentence or join the United States Army. The next day he enlisted in the Army for a three-year stint.

After basic training at Fort Ord near Monterey, California, he was assigned in November 1961 to the legendary 101st Airborne Division at Fort Campbell, Kentucky. Before the year was over, he made his first jump out of an airplane (not only was it Hendrix's first jump, it was also the first time he had ever been in an airplane). In January 1962 he was promoted to private first class. With it came 101st Airborne "Screaming Eagles" patch, something he had long desired and wore with pride.

While practicing his guitar in a service club at Fort Campbell one day, Hendrix caught the attention of a serviceman named Billy Cox. Cox had played bass in a few bands over the years, and before long he and Hendrix were jamming. Soon they brought in three more servicemen and put together a five-piece band that played weekends at clubs on the base.

Hendrix's love for the band was soon at odds with his Army career. Cox was almost done with his Army commitment and ready to make music fulltime. But Hendrix still had more than two years remaining. He decided he wanted out – fast. So, he arranged to meet the base psychiatrist and began to claim all sorts of maladies; dizziness, weight loss, trouble sleeping, night terrors, bed wetting, and chest pains among them. He also said he was in love with someone in his barracks, a claim that was almost certainly a ruse, but one that the Army at that time never liked to hear.

Clearly, this was a man looking for a quick way to put his days in the Army behind him. The remarkable thing was that it worked. He was given a general discharge under honorable conditions on June 29, 1962.

With the Army out of the way, Hendrix could now focus all of his energy on music. He practiced his guitar like a man possessed. In his book *Room Full of Mirrors: A Biography of Jimi Hendrix*, author Charles R. Cross described Hendrix's passion for the instrument: "Practicing his guitar was the central activity in Jimi's life that year. He went to bed practicing, he slept with the guitar on his chest, and the first thing he did upon rising was to start practicing again." Cross went on to say, "The guitar had become an extension of his body." Cross also noted that bandmate

Alphonso Young recalled, "Jimi would practice on the way to a gig, play for up to five hours during one of their all-night shows, and then continue to practice on the car ride home." Billy Cox said Jimi "managed to put twenty-five years into the guitar in a period of just five."

By 1964, his skills had improved to the point that he was touring with the Isley Brothers, who had broken through in 1959 with "Shout," a song that sold a million records. The Isley gig was followed by a stint with Little Richard, who already had several big hits, including "Tutti Frutti," "Long Tall Sally," and "Good Golly, Miss Molly." After that, for a short while, Hendrix played in Ike and Tina Turner's band. He was also finding occasional work as a studio musician.

In 1965, he got his best gig to date touring with Joey Dee and the Starlighters who, a few years earlier, had a number one hit called "Peppermint Twist." When that tour ended, Hendrix hooked up for a few months with saxophonist King Curtis.

Despite all the work he had put into his career up to that point, Hendrix was living, at best, from hand to mouth. His gigs were either short-lived or paid little. He often had to rely on the generosity of friends to slip him a few bucks when he was short on cash or provide him with a place to crash for a time.

But that all began to change in 1966 when Bryan James "Chas" Chandler happened to see Hendrix playing at Café Wha? in Manhattan's Greenwich Village. Hendrix had started going by the name Jimmy James and, at the time, was fronting a band called Jimmy James and the Blue Flames. Chandler was a member of The Animals, a British group formed in the early 1960s with Eric

Burton as the lead singer, which had recorded such huge hits as "The House of the Rising Sun," "It's My Life," "We Gotta Get Out of This Place," and "Don't Let Me Be Misunderstood." Chandler was looking to separate from the band and start a new career in the record business as a manager and producer. When he saw Hendrix doing his thing on stage, he immediately saw a future for them both.

In September 1966, Chandler convinced Hendrix to go with him to England. Chandler and Michael Jeffery, the former manager of The Animals, put together a contract that made them co-managers of Hendrix. At Jeffery's suggestion, he dumped the name Jimmy James and went back to Jimmy Hendrix.

In short order Chandler and Jeffery hired a drummer and a bass player to back up Hendrix. And, at about the same time, Hendrix changed the spelling of his first name to Jimi. The new band would be called The Jimi Hendrix Experience. The rocket was now on the launch pad, fully fueled, and ready to shoot into rock and roll history.

Within just a few months The Jimi Hendrix Experience recorded three singles: "Hey Joe," "Purple Haze," and "The Wind Cries Mary." All were hits. In May 1967, they released their first album in the United Kingdom called "Are You Experienced." It spent 33 weeks on the British charts, peaking at number 2. In 2003, *Rolling Stone* magazine ranked it 15th on their list of 500 greatest albums of all time. In 2005, the Library of Congress included it in a list of 50 recordings selected for that year to be added to the United States National Recording Registry, a list of sound recordings considered "culturally, historically, or aesthetically significant."

Hendrix returned to the United States in 1967 and kicked off a tour by performing at the three-day Monterey International Pop Festival held in Monterey, California, from Friday, June 16th, to Sunday, June 18th. On the final night, Hendrix finished his set with "Wild Thing." When the song ended, he poured lighter fluid on his guitar and set it on fire. Before leaving the stage, he smashed the flaming guitar into bits and tossed the splinters into the stunned audience.

In December 1967, the Experience released in the United Kingdom their second album, titled "Axis: Bold as Love." A month later it was released in the United States. It soon reached the Top Ten in both countries. *Rolling Stone* ranked it 83rd on their greatest-albums list in 2003.

In 1968, Hendrix and Michael Jeffrey came up with the idea of opening a club of their own. They jumped right in and leased a venue at 52 West 8th Street in the Manhattan's Greenwich Village. The address had previously housed the recently closed Generation Club, a place Hendrix was familiar with because it often attracted big names like B.B. King, Chuck Berry, Janis Joplin, Dave Van Ronk, and Sly and the Family Stone. Jimi sometimes would jam with the visiting talent.

The three-story building had a long history. It had been designed by famed architect Frederick Kiesler and built about 1927. Its first tenant was the Film Guild Cinema, a theater/cinema that was later renamed the 8th Street Playhouse. In November 1930, the basement was made into a popular country and western venue called the Village Barn. The club had a long run there, closing in August of 1967, but not before the first live country music program

The Electric Lady Studio as it looks today. (Photo by author)

on American network television was broadcast weekly from there by NBC-TV from May 1948 to May 1950. The artist Hans Hoffman also had a connection to the address; he had a unit in the building and taught there from 1938 to 1958.

When studio engineer Eddie Kramer was looking over the newly purchased venue, he suggested to Hendrix and Jeffrey that their money would be much better spent by turning the place into a recording studio. Considering that Hendrix was spending $150,000 (over a million dollars today) each year in recording-studio fees, it apparently didn't take much prodding to convince both new entrepreneurs that a recording studio made a lot more financial sense than a club. Work got started on a studio right away.

Hendrix's third album, "Electric Ladyland," was released in October 1968. In November it went to number 1 on the U.S. charts and spent two weeks at the top. In 2003, it was ranked 55th on *Rolling Stone* magazine's greatest album list. It included "All Along the Watchtower," a song written by Bob Dylan, which was released as a single. That song reached number 20 in the U.S. charts, making it the best-selling single ever by the Experience.

By mid-1969, the stresses of touring and recording had taken its toll on the band. They broke up after playing at the Denver Pop Festival in June. Jimi moved to a house near Woodstock, New York. It was while there that he got invited to be the closing act at Woodstock, officially called The Woodstock Music and Art Fair, to be held in nearby Bethel, New York. Jimi quickly put together a new band he called Gypsy Sun and Rainbows. He was paid $18,000 for the gig (about $150,000 today), more than any of the other acts at Woodstock.

The three-day festival was scheduled to run from Friday, August 15th through Sunday, August 17th, with Jimi penciled in to play at 11 pm Sunday. But because of countless delays he didn't walk onto the stage until about 8 a.m. Monday morning. Of the estimated 400,000 people who were there just two days before, only about 40,000 remained. Jimi's set consisted of 16 songs, but the one most famously remembered was his take on "The Star-Spangled Banner." At the time, the *New York Post* observed: "It was the most electrifying moment of Woodstock, and it was probably the single greatest moment of the sixties." *Guitar World* magazine called it the greatest performance of all time.

After a number of delays that stretched the build-time to two years, Jimi's recording studio was finally completed in August of 1970. He named it Electric Lady Studios. He wanted a place that encouraged maximum creativity, so everything it in was built to his specifications. The color of the lights could be instantly changed to match Jimi's mood that day. Psychedelic paintings reflected the current trend in art. The addition of round windows and curved walls made for better acoustics. And the control room was made extra-large, unusual at that time, so the artists and engineers would have plenty of room to collaborate side-by-side at the mixing console.

The studio was officially opened on August 26th. Eric Clapton, Patti Smith, Ron Wood, and Steve Winwood were among the guests that showed up to help celebrate the event.

The next day Jimi used the studio to record the instrumental "Slow Blues." It was the last recording he ever made. He left for England less than 24 hours later.

On Sunday, August 30th, Jimi played to an estimated 600,000 to 700,000 people at the Isle of Wight Festival in England. Yes, it was bigger than Woodstock. He then began a European tour that brought him on September 6th to the Isle of Fehmarn Festival in Germany, where he played in front of 25,000 people. It would be his final concert.

Jimi returned to London, staying at the Samarkand Hotel with his girlfriend. Sometime during the early morning of September 18th, unable to sleep after taking a mix of drugs and drinking wine the night before, Jimi took several sleeping pills, a dose far beyond what would be considered safe. At some point he vomited and aspirated some of the contents into his lungs, causing him to choke to death. He was 27 years old. He was buried in his hometown of Seattle.

Jimi's untimely passing didn't signal a death knell for the Electric Lady Studio. Other musicians were soon booking time there. Not only did Electric Lady provide them with a state-of-the-art studio, it also came filled with all the good vibrations that Jimi Hendrix put into the place.

Some of the talent that has spent time there include Adele, Beyonce, Billie Idol, Blondi, Bob Dylan, David Bowie, Daft Punk, John Batist, Kanye West, Kiss, Lady Gaga, Lana Del Rey, Led Zeppelin, Lorde, Lou Reed, Madonna, Patti Smith, Run DMC, Ryan Adams, Stevie Wonder, Taylor Swift, The Clash, The Roots, and U2. Over the years the Electric Lady Studio has been upgraded and modernized, but despite those changes, Jimi's mojo still permeates the air there as much as it did in 1970.

The Cotton Club

It's been called the most famous nightclub in American history, and, during the Jazz Age of the 1920s and 1930s, it was the place to be in Manhattan for those seeking music, dance, entertainment, and illegal booze.

Location (1923 to 1935): 644 Lenox Avenue
Nearest subway stop: 145th Street Station/Lenox Avenue
Location (1936 to 1940): 200 West 48th Street
Nearest subway stop: 49th Street Station/7th Avenue

....

Go back in time to Manhattan a hundred years ago, and you would soon discover that anyone with a decent arm could throw a stone in any direction and likely hit a spot where people were gathered to enjoy illegal booze. Such places were called speakeasies, a name that probably came about because customers would talk in hushed tones, or "speak easy," whenever the establishment was mentioned, a collective effort by the clientele to keep the place unknown by authorities.

There was nothing new in the history of the United States about businesses selling illegal spirits, although the practice was traditionally relatively uncommon. All that began to change on December 18, 1917, when Congress passed the Eighteenth Amendment to the Constitution. Section 1 of the Amendment told most of the story: "After one year from the ratification of this article, the manufacture, sale, or transportation of intoxicating liquors within, the importation thereof into, or the exportation thereof from the United States and all territory subject to the jurisdiction thereof for beverage purposes is hereby prohibited."

Thirteen months later, on January 16, 1919, the Amendment was ratified after it received approval from the required three-fourths of the states. In preparation for implementing it, Congress passed the National Prohibition Act on October 28, 1919. More commonly known as the Volstead Act – named after Andrew John Volstead, a Republican Congressman from Minnesota – it spelled out in detail how the law would work. On January 17, 1920, one year after the Eighteenth Amendment was ratified, it became the law of the land.

But prohibition on paper didn't necessarily mean prohibition in practice. Many Americans, including a good number of its polite citizens – schoolteachers, grocery clerks, factory workers, police officers, politicians, judges, doctors, accountants, and many others – still wanted to enjoy the occasional tipple. So, no sooner had the ink dried on the document, speakeasies began popping up overnight almost everywhere.

Indeed, it has been estimated that across all five boroughs of New York City during prohibition, there were between 20,000 and 100,000 such watering holes. Some were little more than oversized closets, while others rivaled the size and entertainment chops of a Broadway theater.

Among the most famous of these was an establishment in Harlem called The Cotton Club. Compared to just about all other speakeasys in Manhattan at the time, it stood out like a polished diamond in a box of rocks. Its popularity even extended across the Atlantic Ocean. After a visit to Harlem by Lady Mountbatten (the wife of Lord Mountbatten, great-grandson to Queen Victoria), she proclaimed the Cotton Club to be "The Aristocrat of Harlem." Not to be outdone, Maurice Chevalier, the famous French singer, said at the time that the Cotton Club was "the most sophisticated café in New York."

The roots of the club go back to 1918 when a place called The Douglas Casino was opened in what had been a dance hall over a movie theater at 644 Lenox Avenue between West 142nd Street and West 143rd Street. Then, in 1920, 45-year-old Jack Johnson, the famous African-American ex-heavyweight boxing champion, leased the venue and converted it into a 400-seat supper club. He called it Club Deluxe.

In 1923, with the venue struggling financially, Johnson sold it to Owen Madden, a powerful New York gangster everyone called Owney. At the time, Madden – once the leader of the infamous

The Cotton Club at its original location, circa 1930, on Lennox Avenue in Harlem. (Wikimedia Commons)

Gopher Gang from the Hell's Kitchen neighborhood – was about to get out of prison after serving seven years of a 10- to 20-year sentence for manslaughter.

Madden had likely never been on a farm, but he could certainly recognize a cash cow. In short order he was working as a successful bootlegger and, before long, had his own brand of beer, brazenly labeling it "Madden's No. 1 Beer." It was made at his own brewery on 26th Street. He not only sold it at the Cotton Club, he also delivered barrels of it around New York City and New Jersey. At a time when most illegally made beer was considered swill, thirsty

When this photo was taken in 1927, the Cotton Club was just one of several businesses that filled out the block at the corner of Lenox Avenue and West 142nd Street. (Wikimedia Commons)

customers claimed his product hit the spot like no other. All of a sudden, Owney Madden was making some serious cash.

Now that he owned Club Deluxe, Madden had big ideas for the Lenox Avenue venue. The first thing he did was change the name to the Cotton Club. Then he expanded the seating to accommodate 700 people and added a horseshoe-shaped stage. All the seats were arranged to wrap around a generously sized dance floor that could double as a show floor.

Madden next began hiring some of the best African-American musicians, singers, and dancers to work there. Duke Ellington, Cab Calloway, Lena Horne, Bill "Bojangles" Robertson, and Louis Armstrong were just a few of the ultra-talented people who spent time at the place.

To Madden's credit, he made sure the entertainers were well paid, and, in return, they put together performances that made the Cotton Club the envy of every other club in town. Female dancers had to be light-skinned and knock-out beautiful, and in the typically skimpy outfits they were required to wear, they made the stage about as hot as the Lenox Street sidewalk on a mid-July afternoon.

The Cotton Club has often been described as a whites-only club, but that's not exactly true. It didn't become fully segregated until it moved downtown to Times Square in 1936. While at Lenox Avenue from 1923 to 1935, anyone properly dressed – white or black – could get inside after paying the $4 cover charge. That said, a $4 charge in 1926 would be equal to about $70 today. And that was just to get a seat at a table. First you had to pay to check your coat and hat and then buy booze and, if hungry, have dinner while there.

A quart of orange juice was $5 ($85 today; customers supplied the alcohol from their own pocket flask). Although dinner prices were not completely unreasonable – a sirloin steak was $2 ($35 today) and Chicken Chow Mein from their Chinese menu was $1 ($17.50 today) – a party of four that included tips for the waiter and hat check girl could easily spend the equivalent of $600 for a night at the club. For the average African-American living in Harlem, that was way beyond their pay scale. For that matter, it was way beyond what most white middle-class New Yorkers could afford.

But the Cotton Club never had a problem filling up tables. The men and women that showed up every night mostly came from toney areas downtown. Often seen stepping out of limousines, they came uptown to enjoy the remarkable talent and illegal booze, and to absorb the exotic sights and sounds and flavors of Harlem, all from the safe vantage point of a comfortable table not far from the stage. And come they did, relishing every aspect of the place: the music, the shows, the beautiful girls, and Madden's tasty beer. All the while, Madden's deep pockets ensured that the authorities looked the other way.

A show at the Cotton Club was usually a musical revue that included dancers, singers, comedians, and variety acts. The shows normally ran twice each night, at midnight and 2 am. The stage sets typically had a theme based on the Antebellum period in the South. While working there, band leader Cab Calloway described one of his stage sets:

> The bandstand was a replica of a southern mansion, with large
> white columns and a backdrop painted with weeping willows

and slave quarters. The band played on the veranda of the mansion, and in front of the veranda, down a few steps, was the dance floor, which was also used for the show . . . the whole set was like sleepytime-down-South during slavery. Even the name, Cotton Club, was supposed to convey that southern feeling. I suppose the idea was to make the whites who came to the club feel like they were catered to and entertained by black slaves.

Naturally, many African-Americans were offended by the way they were depicted in the shows. Author Langston Hughes was one of them. In his 1940 autobiography he bluntly said: "Nor did ordinary Negroes like the growing influx of whites toward Harlem after sundown, flooding the little cabarets and bars where formerly only colored people laughed and sang, and where now the strangers were given the best ringside tables to sit and stare at the Negro customers – like amusing animals in a zoo." Hughes had it about right. Much of the Cotton Club's success was based on a wildly inaccurate characterization of an entire race of people.

The earliest "house band" at the Cotton Club was called Wilson Robinson's Syncopators. Robinson, an African-American violinist from St. Louis, assembled The Syncopators in the early 1920s while living in the Midwest. From there the band moved to Chicago before receiving an invite to the Cotton Club in 1925. Once in New York, violinist Andy Preer took over as leader of the band and soon they were being billed as The Cotton Club Orchestra.

When Andy Peer died in 1927, he was replaced by 29-year-old Edward Kennedy "Duke" Ellington, a remarkably talented pianist, composer, and recording artist who had his own orchestra.

Ellington would go on to become the greatest jazz composer and bandleader of his era. Indeed, during his lifetime he composed more than 3,000 songs. Ellington's five-year tenure at the Cotton Club was time well spent as it allowed him to expand and polish his already considerable skills. While there, many of his performances were broadcast nationally on radio station WHN. Some were even recorded and released on albums. Thanks to the Cotton Club, it didn't take long for Duke Ellington to become famous from Connecticut to California. His orchestra remained as the house band until he moved on in 1931 and was replaced by Cab Calloway.

At the time, Calloway – a talented singer, drummer, pianist, and dancer – was the front man for the Missourians, a popular jazz band that had evolved from Wilson Robinson's Syncopators. Once at the Cotton Club, the Missourians were given a new name – The Cab Calloway Orchestra. The band would appear regularly at the Cotton Club until 1940. Calloway is perhaps best known for his song "Minnie the Moocher." The recording sold a million copies – the first time an African-American broke that mark – and would be his signature song for the rest of his career.

The Cotton Club was doing just fine until Tuesday, March 19, 1935. Early that afternoon, a 16-year-old Puerto Rican boy was caught stealing a penknife at Kress's Five and Dime store on 125th Street in Harlem. Police were called, but the store manager didn't want to press charges, so the boy was released after being taken downstairs and shown the back door. However, rumors soon began circulating that the police had beaten the boy. They hadn't. Soon after, the driver of a hearse just happened to park his vehicle nearby in order to visit his brother, who worked at Kress's. When a gathering crowd spotted the hearse, they concluded that the boy had died.

This prompted someone to throw a rock through Kress's window. As the shattered glass fell to the sidewalk, it signaled the start of a full-blown riot. When the sun came up the next morning, almost 700 plate-glass windows in Harlem were broken. Some 300 businesses were affected. It was estimated that more than 3,000 people took to the streets that night, although most of them behaved peacefully. The injured included 57 civilians and 7 police officers. In all the confusion, an African-American boy who was walking home from a movie was shot and killed by the police. Three

The Cotton Club, circa 1937, after it moved downtown to Times Square. (Science History Images)/Alamy Stock Photo)

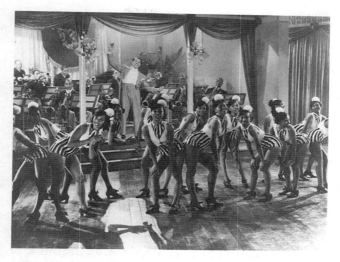

Cab Calloway and his dancers performing at the Time Square location, circa 1937. (Wikimedia Commons)

other African-Americans would also die before everything settled down.

The riot stunned New Yorkers, both white and African American. Virtually overnight, for many whites, Harlem became a place that was best avoided. The Cotton Club took note. Before the year 1935 was over, it had relocated downtown, just a few blocks north of Times Square at 200 West 48th Street.

The new venue came with several changes. For starters, it was bigger. Then, too, Owney Madden was no longer the owner – he had left the club a couple of years earlier. Also, it had a new house band – Andy Kirk and his Clouds of Joy. And because the Eighteenth Amendment had been repealed in 1933, liquor was once again legal to drink anywhere. Most significantly, however, for the first time since opening in 1923, the Cotton Club was now strictly segregated. That's right: in Times Square in Manhattan, in the year

1935, the Cotton Club featured talent that was 100 percent African American but not a single African-American customer was allowed in the seats. In short, Manhattan's Cotton Club was as segregated as any place in the deep south.

As it turned out, the West 48th Street location was not a great one for the Cotton Club. After just five years there, it closed its doors for good. Several things led to the club's demise. For one, the Times Square location lacked the perceived adventure and danger that had given the Harlem venue its special mojo. The thrill of flaunting the law at a comfortable dinner table in the Cotton Club was lost when booze became as legit as lemonade. Also, the music of Andy Kirk began to feature less jazz and more waltzes, so the shows

The Lenox Avenue location today. (Photo by author)

felt less like a Harlem production and more like Broadway. Finally, the United States was in the middle of the Great Depression, and money was tight even for the wealthy. Add it all up and that was a lot of baggage for a supper club to carry. It closed for good on June 10, 1940.

The building that housed the Cotton Club in Harlem at 644 Lenox Avenue between 1923 and 1935 was torn down in the fall

The Times Square location today. (Photo by author)

of 1958 to make room for a housing complex. Visit the location today you'll find a 15-story apartment building and, next door, the Minisink Townhouse of the NY Mission Society, a community-based nonprofit charged with helping kids and families overcome the challenges of poverty.

The building at 200 West 48th Street in Times Square, where the Cotton Club was located between 1936 and 1940, was torn down in 1989. A hotel was put up in its place. Today at the West 48th Street address you'll find the north-facing side of the Renaissance New York Times Square Hotel, although the actual address of the hotel faces east at 714 Seventh Avenue.

Manhattan saw sweeping social and cultural changes during the 17-year history of the Cotton Club and was fundamentally altered by the ups and downs of the Harlem renaissance, the jazz age, Prohibition, the stock market crash and, finally, the Great Depression. Indeed, it was the ups of the Harlem renaissance and jazz age that gave the club the jump start it needed. Prohibition provided plenty of energy to keep it going. Unfortunately, the downs sucked the Cotton Club of all its vitality until the place could run no more.

During its relatively short life, the Cotton Club became an entertainment venue rarely matched in either musical style or substance. It produced shows that dazzled the eyes and ears of New Yorkers who had never imagined such sights and sounds. Regrettably, it was also tainted by deeply racist policies and practices. However, for a handful of talented African-Americans, the Cotton Club provided a place like no other to showcase their skills as musicians, composers, singers, dancers, and comedians, many of whom remain icons to this day.

Selected Notes

The Battle of Fort Washington

Burrows, Edwin G., *Forgotten Patriots: The Untold Story of American Prisoners During the Revolutionary War*, Basic Books, New York, 2008.

Duffus, R.L., *Traitor Caused the Loss of New York,* New York Times, November 14, 1926. www.nytimes.com/1926/11/14/archives/traitor-caused-the-loss-of-new-york-capture-of-fort-washington.html?searchResultPosition=1

Fort Washington: An Account of the Identification of the Site of Fort Washington, New York City, and the Erection and Dedication of a Monument thereon Nov. 16, 1901, The Empire State Society of the Sons of the American Revolution, 1902, New York.

Hall, Edward Hagaman, *Margaret Corbin: Heroine of the Battle of Fort Washington, 16 November 1776*, The American Scenic and Historic Preservation Society, 1932, New York.

Lapp, Derrick E., *The Fall of Fort Washington: The "Bunker Hill Effect"?*, Journal of the American Revolution, July 7, 2020. www.allthingsliberty.com/2020/07/the-fall-of-fort-washington-the-bunker-hill-effect

Michals, Debra, PhD, *Margaret Cochran Corbin, 1751-1800*, National Women's History Museum, 2015. www.womenshistory.org/education-resources/biographies/margaret-cochran-corbin

O'Malley, Brian Patrick, *1776—The Horror Show*, Journal of the American Revolution, January 29, 2019. www.allthingsliberty.com/2019/01/1776-the-horror-show

Schenawolf, Harry, *The Battle of Fort Washington was the Final Devastating Chapter in George Washington's Disastrous New York Campaign*, Revolutionary War Journal, July 29, 2019. www.revolutionarywarjournal. com/the-battle-of-fort-washington-was-the-final-devastating-chapter-in-george-washingtons-disastrous-new-york-campaign

Tom's Restaurant

Armstrong, Jennifer Keishin, *Seinfeldia: How a Show About Nothing Changed Everything*, Simon and Schuster, New York, 2016.

Divola, Barry, *The real Seinfeld diner in New York: Inside Tom's Restaurant*, Traveler online, February 28, 2016. www.traveller.com.au/the-seinfeld-diner-gn0ydp

Sablich, Justin, *A Food Tour of Seinfeld's New York*, The New York Times, June 23, 2015.

Samuel, Benjamin, *Checking in on the "Seinfeld" Diner 21 Years Later*, Inside Hook, July 12, 2019. www.insidehook.com/article/food-drink-new-york/review-checking-in-on-the-seinfeld-diner-21-years-later-toms-manhattan

Zeller, Jonathan, *In Honor of Seinfeld's 30th Anniversary, We Visited Tom's Restaurant (Which Sometimes Has a Big Salad)*, NYC: The Official Guide, July 3, 2019. www.nycgo.com/articles/seinfeld-30th-anniversary-toms-restaurant-kenny-kramer-hh-bagels

The Rock Outcrop Where Edgar Allan Poe Loved to Sit and Think

Geiling, Natasha, *The (Still) Mysterious Death of Edgar Allan Poe*, Smithsonian Magazine. October 7, 2014. www.smithsonianmag.com/history/still-mysterious-death-edgar-allan-poe-180952936/

Harrison, James A., *Life of Edgar Allan Poe*, Thomas Y. Crowell, New York, 1902, 1903.

Morgan, Appleton, Dr., *Edgar Allen Poe in New York*, Valentine's Manual of Old New York, Number 7, Brown, Henry Collins (editor), Valentine's Manual, Inc., 1923, pg. 263

Quinn, Arthur Hobson, *Edgar Allan Poe, A Critical Biography*, D. Appleton-Century Company, New York, London, 1941.

Thomas, Dwight and Jackson, David K, *The Poe Log: A Documentary Life of Edgar Allan Poe, 1809-1849*, G.K. Hall & Co., Boston, 1987. www.eapoe.org/papers/misc1921/tplg00ca.htm

Woodberry, George E., *Edgar Allan Poe,* The Riverside Press, Cambridge, 1885

The First Pedestrian Killed by an Automobile in the United States Happened Here

Haberman, Clyde, *NYC; Marking Birth of Death On the Road,* The New York Times, September14, 1999.

Kat, Eschner, *Henry Bliss, America's First Pedestrian Fatality, Was Hit by an Electric Taxi*, Smithsonian Magazine, September 13, 2017. www.smithsonianmag.com/smart-news/henry-bliss-americas-first-pedestrian-fatality-was-hit-electric-taxi-180964852/

The 'Death Stretch' Beside the Park, New York Journal and Advertiser, September 15, 1899). www.loc.gov/resource/sn83030180/1899-09-15/ed-1/?sp=7&r=0.235,-0.086,0.927,0.399,0

Williams, Keith, *Who Was the First Person Killed by a Car in New York?*, The New York Times, March 30, 2018.

Where Dustin Hoffman Yelled at a Cabby, "Hey! I'm Walkin' Here!"

Biskind, Peter, *Midnight Revolution*, Vanity Fair, April 8, 2010. www.vanityfair.com/hollywood/2010/04/midnight-revolution-200503

Cronin, Brian, *Movie Legends: The Truth Behind the Famous "I'm Walkin' Here" Scene*, CBR.com, October 15, 2017. www.cbr.com/midnight-cowbody-im-walkin-here

Knight, Chris, *"Hey, I'm walkin' here:" Dustin Hoffman explains his famous Midnight Cowboy ad-lib*, nationalpost.com, September 10, 2012.

Audrey Hepburn Had Her Breakfast at Tiffany's Here

Audrey Hepburn's Little Black Dress Sells For A Fortune, hellomagazine.com, December 6, 2006. www.hellomagazine.com/celebrities/2006/12/06/audrey-hepburn-dress

Gene Moore, master of Tiffany's windows, died on November 23rd, aged 88, The Economist, December 10, 1998. www.economist.com/obituary/1998/12/10/gene-moore

Hanks E.A., *Holly Golightly Is a Call Girl and Other Revelations About Breakfast at Tiffany's*, Vanity Fair, June 22, 2010. www.vanityfair.com/culture/2010/06/holly-golightly-is-a-call-girl-and-other-revelations-about-breakfast-at-tiffanys

Horsley, Carter B., *The Tiffany Building*, thecityreview.com. (no date). www.thecityreview.com/tiffb.html

The Magical Windows of Tiffany, Tiffany & Co. (no date). www.tiffany.com/world-of-tiffany/windows-of-tiffany

Where a Hail of Hot Lead Cut Down Mob Boss Albert Anastasia

Berger, Meyer, *Anastasia Slain in a Hotel Here, Led Murder Inc.*, The New York Times, October, 26, 1957. https://www.nytimes.com/1957/10/26/archives/anastasia-slain-in-a-hotel-here-led-murder-inc-victims-brothers.html?searchResultPosition=1

Dunlap, David W., *Hint: It Wasn't the Orange Crème Frappucino*, The New York Times, October 25, 2007. https://archive.nytimes.com/cityroom.blogs. nytimes.com/2007/10/25/hint-it-wasnt-the-orange-creme-frappucino/ ?searchResultPosition=1

Hunt, Thomas, *Anastasia delayed, did not escape death in 'chair,'* writersofwrongs. com, October 25, 2019. www.writersofwrongs.com/2019/10/anastasia-delayed-did-not-escape-death.html

Suit Against Anastasia; U. S. Begins Action to Quash Citizenship of Albert, The New York Times, December 30, 1953. https://www.nytimes.com/ search?query=Suit+Against+Anastasia%3B+U.+S.+Begins+Action+to+ Quash+Citizenship+of+Albert%2C+

The Disco Where the World's Beautiful People Danced the Night Away

Dowd, Vincent, *Studio 54: "The best party of your life,"* BBC News (bbc.com), April 26, 2012. www.bbc.com/news/magazine-17829308

Flynn, Paul, *The inside story of Studio 54, New York's most legendary club ever*, British GQ magazine (gq-magazine.co.uk), July 21, 2020. www. gq-magazine.co.uk/culture/article/studio-54

Romeyn, Kathryn, *Studio 54's Paradigm-Shifting Design*, Architectural Digest (architecturaldigest.com), October 2, 2018. www.architecturaldigest. com/story/studio-54-documentary-design

What happened at Studio 54 is still an "embarrassment" for co-founder Ian Schrager, CBS News (cbsnews.com), October 13, 2018. www.cbsnews. com/news/studio-54-cofounder-ian-schrager-what-happened-at-studio-54-is-still-an-embarrassment

Marilyn Dazzled Us Here

Desta, Yohana, *The Untold story Behind an Iconic Marilyn Monroe Moment*, Vanity Fair (vanityfair.com), January 13, 2017. www.vanityfair.com/hollywood/2017/01/marilyn-monroe-rare-footage

Marilyn Monroe films famous flying skirt scene in New York, New York Daily News, September 16, 1954. www.nydailynews.com/entertainment/movies/marilyn-monroe-famous-skirt-scene-filmed-new-york-1954-article-1.2792234?gclid=CjwKCAiAsIDxBRAsEiwAV76N82y07g VXaf1wlf-pps4SMLYHOcRRpRde84Q-CbXWtL75NQupK6dgrxo CXm4QAvD_BwE

Schwarz, Ted, *Marilyn Revealed: The Ambitious Life of an American Icon*, Taylor Trade Publishing, Lanham, Md., 2009.

Stevens, Melissa, *Behind-the-Scenes of Marilyn Monroe's Iconic Flying Skirt*, Biography (biography.com), September 14, 2014. www.biography.com/news/marilyn-monroe-seven-year-itch-dress-photos#comments

Tin Pan Alley: the Birthplace of American Popular Music

Bluebook of Pianos, *U.S. Piano Sales History, Brand New Pianos Sold From 1900 to Present*. www.bluebookofpianos.com/uspiano.htm

Colangelo, Lisa L. and Pereira, Ivan, *Tin Pan Alley on West 28th Street could become an NYC landmark*, AMNY (amny.com), March 12, 2019. www.amny.com/news/tin-pan-alley-landmark-1.28432646. https://ny.curbed.com/2019/12/10/21004775/tin-pan-alley-landmarks-preservation-commission-designation-west-28th-street

Jasen, David A, *Tin Pan Alley: an encyclopedia of the golden age of American song*, Routledge/Taylor and Francis Books, New York, London, 2003.

Mierisch, Fred, *In Tin Pan Alley*, The New York Times, February 18, 1923. https://timesmachine.nytimes.com/timesmachine/1923/02/18/105848547.html?pageNumber=150

New York Historic Districts Council, *A Brief-ish History of Tin Pan Alley*, March 12, 2019. www.hdc.org/policy/a-brief-ish-history-of-tin-pan-alley-policy

Ricciulli, Valeria, *Tin Pan Alley buildings are now NYC landmarks,* Curbed New York (ny.curbed.com), December 10, 2019.

The First Oreo Cookie Was Baked Here

Bagli, Charles V., *$2.4 Billion Deal for Chelsea Market Enlarges Google's New York Footprint*, The New York Times, February 7, 2018. https://www.nytimes.com/2018/02/07/nyregion/google-chelsea-market-new-york.html?searchResultPosition=1

Bhardwaj, Prachi, *A historical dive into Google's new New York property, Chelsea Market,* Insider (businessinsider.com), February 18, 2018. www.businessinsider.com/history-of-new-york-city-google-property-chelsea-market-2018-2

Cahn, William, *Out of the cracker barrel; the Nabisco story, from animal crackers to zuzus,* Simon and Schuster, New York, 1969.

Eber, Hailey, *The Big O*, New York Post, February 26, 2012. www.nypost.com/2012/02/26/the-big-o

Gray, Christopher, *From Oreos and Mallomars to Today's Chelsea Market*, The New York Times, August 7, 2005. https://www.nytimes.com/2005/08/07/realestate/from-oreos-and-mallomars-to-todays-chelsea-market.html

Thomas' English Muffins Got Started Here

About Thomas.' www.thomasbreads.com/about

FoodReference.com, *Muffins: A History.* www.foodreference.com/html/artmuffinhistory.html

Myers, Dan, *In England, English muffins are just called 'muffins,'* Los Angeles Times, February 2, 2018. www.latimes.com/food/sns-dailymeal-1869637-

eat-england-english-muffins-are-just-called-muffins-20180202-story. html

Nonko, Emily, *There's an Historic English Muffin Oven Hiding Underneath This Chelsea Co-op*, 6sqft (6sqft.com), October 8, 2015, www.6sqft.com/theres-a-historic-english-muffin-oven-hiding-underneath-this-chelsea-co-op

Vasquez, Emily, *Do You Know the Muffin Man Was on West 20th Street?*, The New York Times, July 28, 2006. https://www.nytimes.com/2006/07/28/nyregion/do-you-know-the-muffin-man-was-on-west-20th-street.html? searchResultPosition=1

The Triangle Shirtwaist Company Fire

Hoenig, John M., *The Triangle Fire of 1911*, History Magazine, April/May 2005. www.web.archive.org/web/20060218142702/http://www.fisheries.vims.edu/hoenig/pdfs/Triangle.pdf

Keller, Lisa, *Triangle Shirtwaist Fire*, Museum of the City of New York (mcny.org), November 14, 2016. https://www.mcny.org/story/triangle-shirtwaist-fire

Remembering the 1911 Triangle Factory Fire, Cornell University Kheel Center, January 2011. https://trianglefire.ilr.cornell.edu/

Triangle Shirtwaist Factory Fire, History (history.com), December 2, 2009. www.history.com/topics/early-20th-century-us/triangle-shirtwaist-fire

von Drehle, David, *Uncovering the History of the Triangle Shirtwaist Fire*, Smithsonian Magazine, August, 2006. www.smithsonianmag.com/history/uncovering-the-history-of-the-triangle-shirtwaist-fire-124701842

The General Slocum Steamboat Fire

1,000 Lives May Be Lost in Burning of the Excursion Boat Gen. Slocum, The New York Times, June 16, 1904. https://timesmachine.nytimes.com/timesmachine/1904/06/16/issue.html

Horror in East River, New-York Tribune, June 16, 1904. https://chroniclingamerica. loc.gov/lccn/sn83030214/1904-06-16/ed-1/seq-1/

King, Gilbert, *A Spectacle of Horror – The Burning of the General Slocum*, Smithsonian Magazine, February 21, 2012.

Northrop, Henry Davenport, *New York's Awful Steamboat Horror*, D.Z. Howell publisher, Washington, D.C., 1904.

The General Slocum and Little Germany (exhibit), The New York Historical Society (nyhistory.org), 2004. www.nyhistory.org/exhibitions/general-slocum-and-little-germany

Wingfield, Valerie, *The General Slocum Disaster of June 15, 1904 (blog)*, New York Public Library, June 13, 2011. www.nypl.org/blog/2011/06/13/great-slocum-disaster-june-15-1904

Ghostbuster's Headquarters

Ghostbusters, Wikipedia. *https://www.en.wikipedia.org/wiki/Ghostbusters*

Grundhauser, Eric, *The Tribeca Fire Station That Got a Starring Role in Ghostbusters*, Atlas Obscura (atlasobscura.com), December 9, 2015. www.atlasobscura.com/articles/the-tribeca-fire-station-that-got-a-starring-role-in-ghostbusters

Remembering September, 11, 2001, Lt. Vincent Gerard Halloran, Legacy.com, November 7, 2001. www.legacy.com/sept11/story.aspx?personid=128619

The 1904 Hook and Ladder Company No. 8 – 14 North Moore Street, Daytonian in Manhattan, November 8, 2011. www.daytoninmanhattan.blogspot.com/2011/11/1904-hook-and-ladder-company-no-8-14.html

Where Joe Gallo Got Whacked

Aronson, Harvey, *The Killing of Joey Gallo*, Putnam Books, New York, 1973

Faso, Frank and Kirkman, Edward, *Mob boss Joe Gallo (Crazy Joe) is killed while celebrating his birthday at a Little Italy restaurant in 1972*, New York Daily News, April 8, 1972. www.nydailynews.com/new-york/nyc-crime/crazy-joe-killed-italy-restaurant-1972-article-1.2171636

Gage, Nicholas, *Story of Joe Gallo's murder: 5 in Colombo gang implicated*, The New York Times. May 3,1972. https://www.nytimes.com/1972/05/03/archives/story-of-joe-gallos-murder-5-in-colombo-gang-implicated-informant.html?searchResultPosition=1

Wilson, Michael, *After 4 Decades, Memory of a Mob Killing Still Draws Gawkers*, The New York Times, September 6, 2013. https://www.nytimes.com/2013/09/07/nyregion/after-4-decades-memory-of-a-mob-killing-still-draws-gawkers.html

America's First Pizza Joint

Bernstein, Lenny, *We eat 100 acres of pizza a day in the U.S.*, The Washington Post, January 20, 2015. www.washingtonpost.com/news/to-your-health/wp/2015/01/20/we-eat-100-acres-of-pizza-a-day-in-the-u-s

Daley, Jason, *The Father of American Pizza Is Not Who We Thought He Was*, Smithsonian Magazine, February 8, 2019. www.smithsonianmag.com/smart-news/father-american-pizza-not-who-we-thought-it-was-180971454

Lee, Alexander, *A History of Pizza*, History Today Magazine, Volume 68, Issue 7, July 2018. https://www.historytoday.com/archive/historians-cookbook/history-pizza

Levine, Ed, *Uncovering Pizza's US Origins*, Special Sauce Blog, February 19, 2019. www.thespecialsaucepodcast.com/podcast/special-sauce-uncovering-pizzas-us-origins-1-2

Pomranz, Mike, *New York's Pizza History May Need a Major Rewrite, According to an Upcoming Book*, Food & Wine Magazine, February 6, 2019. https://www.yahoo.com/lifestyle/york-apos-pizza-history-may-174400974.html

The "Bloody Angle" on Chinatown's Doyers Street

Beck, Louis J., *New York's Chinatown, An Historical Presentation Of Its People And Places*, Bohemia Publishing Company, New York, 1898.

Ferranti, Seth, *The Chinese American Gang Wars That Rocked New York*, www.vice.com, July 16, 2016. www.vice.com/en/article/4w5yej/chinese-american-gangs-tong-wars-new-york-chinatown-money-murder

Three Shot Dead in Chinese Theater, The New York Times, August 7, 1905.

Doyers Street Has a Lively Fire, The New York Times, January 11, 1894.

The Nom Wah Tea Parlor

Auffrey, Richard, *Blob Joints: A History of Dim Sum in the U.S.*, passionate foodie.blogspot.com, March 6, 2020. https://passionatefoodie.blogspot.com/2020/03/blob-joints-history-of-dim-sum-in-us.html

Goldfield, Hannah, *The Oldest Restaurant in Manhattan's Chinatown Faces the Coronavirus Shutdown*, The New Yorker magazine, March 20, 2020. www.newyorker.com/magazine/2020/03/30/the-oldest-restaurant-in-manhattans-chinatown-faces-the-coronavirus-shutdown

Hansen, Valerie *The Legacy of the Silk Road*, Yale University, YaleGlobal Online, January 25, 2013.

Mishan, Ligaya, *Nom Wah Tea Parlor*, The New York Times, April 12, 2011.

Spencer, Luke J., *New York's Oldest Dim Sum Restaurant and the Secrets of Chinatown*, Messy Nessy (messynessychic.com), February 13, 2018. www.messynessychic.com/2018/02/13/new-yorks-oldest-dim-sum-restaurant-and-the-secrets-of-chinatown

The Deadly Brooklyn Bridge Pedestrian Stampede

Dead On the New Bridge: Fatal Crush at the Westerly Approach, The New York Times, May 31, 1883.

Crushed On the Bridge: A Frightful Panic Near the New York Anchorage, The Sun, May 31, 1883.

Fatal Panic on Bridge: Crushed and Trampled to Death, New-York Tribune (1893, May 31).

Safety On the Bridge: Precautions Suggested by the Recent Disaster, The New York Times, June 2, 1893.

The Wall Street Bombing

Barron, James, *After 1920 Blast, The Opposite Of 'Never Forget'; No Memorials on Wall St. For Attack That Killed 30*, The New York Times, September 17, 2003. https://www.nytimes.com/2003/09/17/nyregion/after-1920-blast-opposite-never-forget-no-memorials-wall-st-for-attack-that.html?searchResultPosition=3

Bomb Kills 29 and Injures 200, New York Tribune, September 17, 1920.

Gage, Beverly, *The Day Wall Street Exploded*, Oxford University Press, Oxford, 2009

Wall Street Bombing 1920, FBI Famous Cases and Criminals, FBI. www.fbi.gov/history/famous-cases/wall-street-bombing-1920

Wall Street Explosion Kills 30, Injures 300, The New York Times, September 17, 1920.

Alexander Hamilton's Grave

Alexander Hamilton, History (history.com), December 5, 2019. www.history.com/topics/american-revolution/alexander-hamilton

Chernow, Ron, *Alexander Hamilton*, The Penguin Press, New York, 2004.

Hamilton, John C., *Life of Alexander Hamilton*, Houghton, Osgood and Company, Boston, 1879.

Sumner, William Graham, *Alexander Hamilton*, Houghton, Osgood and Company, Boston, 1890.

Tuttle, Mrs. H. Croswell, *History of St. Luke's Church in the City of New York 1820 –1920, Hamilton Grange)*, Appeal Printing Company, New York, 1926. https://babel.hathitrust.org/cgi/pt?id=nyp.334330 91549422&view=1up&seq=13

The Recording Studio Jimi Hendrix Built

Armstrong, Simon, BBC, *Chas Chandler: The man who discovered Jimi Hendrix*, July 17, 2016. www.bbc.com/news/uk-england-tyne-36674986

Campbell, Chad and Kwong, Matt, *Jimi Hendrix's Electric Lady Studio is still an artistic haven*, NPR, August 26, 2020. https://www.npr.org/2020/08/26/906016218/50-years-later-jimi-hendrixs-electric-lady-studios-is-still-an-artistic-haven

Cross, Charles, R., *Room Full of Mirrors: A Biography of Jimi Hendrix*, Hyperion, New York, 2005.

Ingles, Paul, *A look back at Monterey Pop 50-years later*, NPR, June 15, 2017. https://www.npr.org/2017/06/15/532978213/a-look-back-at-monterey-pop-50-years-later

Jimi Hendrix, Biography (biography.com), January 19, 2018. www.biography.com/musician/jimi-hendrix

Jimi Hendrix: The Life and Music of Jimi Hendrix, Masterclass, June 7, 2021. www.masterclass.com/articles/jimi-hendrix-biography

Lawrence, Wade and Parker, Scott, *Jimi Hendrix – 50 years of peace and music*, Bethel Woods Center For the Arts. www.bethelwoodscenter.org/blog/jimi-hendrix

The Cotton Club

Cotton Club, Britannica (britannica.com). www.britannica.com/topic/Cotton-Club

Cotton Club, Wikipedia. https://en.wikipedia.org/wiki/Cotton_Club

Haskins, James, *The Cotton Club*, Random House, New York, 1977

Maryanski, Maureen, *The Aristocrat of Harlem: The Cotton Club*, New-York Historical Society, February 17, 2016. www.nyhistory.org/blogs/the-aristocrat-of-harlem-the-cotton-club

The Legendary Cotton Club in Harlem 1923 To 1935, Harlem World Magazine. www.harlemworldmagazine.com/harlem-history-the-cotton-club

What's on the menu?, New York Public Library, 1938. www.menus.nypl.org/menus/30937

Index

Federalist Party, 158–159, 162
Fleischman, Mark, 56
Fleming, John, W., 107
Fordham University, 25
Forest Hill, 6
Fort Independence, 21
Fort Lee, 2, 6
Fort Monroe, 21
Fort Moultrie, 21
Fort Tryon, 9
Fort Tryon Park, 9
Fort Washington, 2–3, 5–6, 9–10
Fort Washington, Battle of, 1–11
Fort Washington, Monument
    (Memorial), 8, 10
Franklin, Benjamin, 155

G
Gallo, Joe, 114–117
Gangs of New York, The, 118
General Slocum steamboat, 95–110
Generation Club, 173
George Weston, Ltd., 84
Ghostbuster's movie, 111–113
Ginsberg, Allan, 18
Glikas, Tom, 12
Gold Bug, The, 23
Golightly, (Holly) Holiday, 42,
    44–45
Gopher Gang, 181
Grasso, Arthur, 46, 48–49
Grange, The, 160–162
Graton, Major Alexander, 3
Graybill, James Edward, 154
Gypsy Sun and Rainbows, 175

H
Hall, Edward Hagaman, 7
Halloran, Lieutenant Vincent G.,
    113
Hamilton (Musical), 150

Hamilton, Alexander, 150–166
Hamilton, Angelica, 160, 166
Hamilton, Elizabeth Schuyler, 152,
    158
Hamilton, James A., 151
Hamilton, Philip, 160, 164
Hell Gate, 100–101, 103
Hendrix, Jimi, 167–177
Hepburn, Audrey, 41–45
Hip Sing Tong, 122, 131
Hitchcock, Alfred, 18
Hoffman, Dustin, 35–40
Hoffman, Hans, 174
Horne, Lena, 182
Howe, Admiral Richard, 5
Howe, General William, 1, 4, 6
Hughes, Langston, 184
Hydrox, 73

I
Il Telegrafo, 142
Independence Hall, 156
Isle of Fehmarn Festival, Germany,
    176
Isle of Wight Festival, England, 176
Isley Brothers, 171

J
Jefferson, Thomas, 78, 150, 157–159,
    162
Jeffery, Michael, 172
Joey Dee and the Starlighters, 171
John V. Lindsay East River Park, 110
Johnson, Jack, 180
Jones, Gloria Mosolino, 58
Joplin, Janis, 173
J. P. Morgan Company, 144

K
Kansas City Star, 131
Kiesler, Frederick, 173